1|64 (5)

52/6

ENGLISH MASTER PAINTERS

Edited by SIR HERBERT READ

SIR THOMAS LAWRENCE

ENGLISH MASTER PAINTERS

REYNOLDS *by* Ellis K. Waterhouse
BONINGTON *by* The Hon. Andrew Shirley
HOGARTH *by* R. B. Beckett
LELY *by* R. B. Beckett
RICHARD WILSON *by* W. G. Constable

In Preparation

GEORGE STUBBS *by* Basil Taylor

KENNETH GARLICK

SIR THOMAS

LAWRENCE

ROUTLEDGE & KEGAN PAUL

First published in 1954
by Routledge & Kegan Paul Ltd.
Broadway House, 68–74 Carter Lane
London E.C.4
Printed in Great Britain
by Butler & Tanner Ltd.
Frome and London

CONTENTS

LIST OF PLATES

INTRODUCTION

THOMAS LAWRENCE was born at Bristol on the 13th of April 1769. He was fourteenth of the sixteen children of Thomas Lawrence, a Supervisor of Excise, and of Lucy Read his wife. Mrs. Lawrence was connected with the family of Read of Brocket Hall in Herefordshire, but the parentage and family of her husband have not yet been proved. The claim put forward by Samuel Lysons that he was descended from Sir Robert Lawrence the Crusader can no longer be maintained.

Lawrence senior was a showman and a spendthrift, a man of parts but not a man of sense. In the year Thomas was born he forsook the Excise, in which he was well established, for the business of innkeeping. His first venture as landlord of *The White Lion* at Bristol proved a failure, and he moved in 1773 to Devizes, to *The Black Bear*, a reputable coaching inn on the Bath to London road and a recognized halt for the better class of traveller. Here Thomas at about the age of five showed a facility for drawing. He had also a gift for 'spouting' and his father apparently produced him to perform to his guests on frequent occasions. By 1779 he had achieved something like renown as a prodigy who could with equal ease take pencil profiles or recite from memory passages of Milton. In this year Fanny Burney stayed at the inn with the Thrales and described him in her diary as 'a most lovely boy of ten years of age who seems to be not merely the wonder of the family, but of the times for his astonishing skill in drawing'. She records a statement made by Mrs. Lawrence that Sir Joshua Reynolds had pronounced him 'the most promising genius he had ever met' and that William Hoare of Bath intended to send him to Italy with his son, Prince. By meetings of this kind Lawrence grew accustomed early to the manners and conversation of persons of quality and intellect.

The few drawings of the Devizes period that survive are in pencil. They are clearly good likenesses but are remarkable only as being the productions of a boy. The best known, the heads of Lord and Lady Kenyon, were stated by Williams to have been made in 1775,[1] but there is no entry in Lord Kenyon's careful diaries to indicate that he stayed in Devizes before December 1779, the year which seems to have established Lawrence's reputation as a prodigy.

In 1779 the father was declared a bankrupt, and by the November of that year, the family (there were five surviving children) had moved to Oxford. Here Thomas took the

---

[1] D. E. Williams, *Life and Correspondence of Sir Thomas Lawrence, Kt.*, 1831, I, 40.

1

likenesses of more than fifty of 'the most eminent personages', exhibited drawings after Bartolozzi which were much admired, and was commissioned to make a copy of Sir Joshua Reynolds's window at New College.[1] Here also his fame was spread by the publication of an engraving of his portrait by William Hoare. How long the Lawrences stayed in Oxford is not recorded, but early in 1780 they were at Weymouth, and by the end of the year had settled in Bath.   He now began to take likenesses in pastel as well as in pencil— they were still for the most part profiles—for which by 1786 he was charging three guineas a head. His earning capacity was immediately apparent and he was soon the chief support of the family.

Bath was important to Lawrence as a place of introduction to visiting members of London Society and more so as an ambiance which compensated for his lack of schooling. As far as we know he had spent two years between the ages of six and eight, presumably as a boarder, at The Fort, a private school in Bristol, and he may have had occasional tutoring at Devizes. It was the father's boast that his son had never been given a lesson in drawing. At Bath he may have learned the use of pastel from William Hoare. Certainly Thomas Barker and his patron Mr. Spackman gave him some instruction in the use of oils. It is, however, true that in the strict sense he was untutored in any subject. His natural gift would have compelled him to draw wherever he had lived, but Fortune was kind in sending him to Bath. He gained there much more than a technique and a clientèle. Book-shops and print-shops were of a high order, and private collections in and around the city were an epitome of fashionable taste. To these he had easy access. Copies after Raphael, Guido and the Carracci were the pictures he first revered and drew from. Above all the Rubens at Corsham Court excited him, and however much in later years he seemed to favour a romantic mode, Raphael the draughtsman and Rubens the colourist set the standards to which he aspired throughout his life.

He soon began to draw subject pieces in the Italian manner—*Christ Reproving Peter*, *Reuben's application to his Father*, *Haman and Mordecai*—and these, for a time, were praised more highly than his portraits. For a copy in crayons after the version of Raphael's *Transfiguration* in Mr. Hamilton's collection on Lansdowne Hill he received in 1785 the silver gilt palette of the Society of Arts of London.

His first recorded oil painting (1786) was a *Christ bearing the Cross*, eight feet high.

1786–1789

In September 1786 Lawrence, now seventeen, was staying in London and made the astonishingly confident statement in a letter to his mother: 'To any but my own family I certainly should not say this; but excepting Sir Joshua, for the painting of a head, I would risk my reputation with any painter in London.'[2] This implies that he was already taking portraits in oil, but when he moved to London permanently (apparently in the summer of 1787), he proposed himself to the public only as a painter of heads in pastel. He had lodgings in Leicester Fields not far from Sir Joshua Reynolds who encouraged him to call. There seems to be no foundation for the suggestion that he worked for a time in Reynolds's studio, but no doubt the advice of Reynolds and the three months he spent as a student of oil painting at the Royal Academy Schools soon decided him to abandon

---

[1] *Oxford Journal*, 6th November 1779.   [2] Williams, I, 83.

2

pastel almost entirely. He had exhibited seven heads at the Academy of 1787 which received unfavourable notice, and one, *A Lady*, was described by the *Whitehall Evening Post* as 'beneath contempt', having 'a round patch of dirty red-lead by way of damask rose on each cheek'.[1] In 1788 he showed four pastels and one oil, in 1789 four pastels and seven oils, and thereafter one pastel only in the exhibitions of 1790 and 1795. He was sufficiently recognized at this time for Lady Eleanor Butler to enter in her diary in the cottage at Llangollen, 'Monday February 25th [1788] . . . Letter from Miss H. Bowdler dated London 22nd. Lawrence the Painter lives Nº. 41 Jermyn St., St. James, price eight guineas.'[2] His parents, meanwhile, had also moved to London, and Lawrence, established with them in a house in Duke St., St. James's, and with a studio in Jermyn St., had involved himself in a rental and a style of living beyond his means. He believed that his success depended on keeping up appearances but he did not foresee that from this time he would never be able to live within his income.

1789–1800

In 1789 Lawrence exhibited his first full-length portrait, *Lady Cremorne* (Plate 1), a work of astonishing competence and a brilliant approximation to the easy dignity of the late Reynolds. Technically it is of particular interest. While the head and figure are painted carefully and firmly, the paint in the landscape background and the foliage is applied in an uncontrolled and extravagant manner. Throughout his life Lawrence was apt to betray his gift for firm modelling with the brush by carelessness of this kind. There are also in the background passages of an unpleasantly muddy tone and, in view of this, some remarks in a letter from Lawrence to Mr. Mulvany of the Royal Hibernian Academy, written thirty-two years later, in November 1821, are relevant here: 'I thank you for your obliging attention in sending me the lists of artists, and now proceed to answer your enquiry respecting the palette. My advice certainly is that you should not mix *tints* upon it. Blend them, for your immediate purpose, with the pencil. In my earlier practice, I did the former; but you have the very highest authority for the latter—that of Sir Joshua Reynolds whose palette was very simple.'[3]

Lady Cremorne, presumably on the strength of this portrait, persuaded Queen Charlotte, somewhat against her will, to sit to Lawrence in the same year. He was summoned to Windsor on 27th September and exhibited the Queen's portrait (Plate 2) with a small three-quarters of the Princess Amelia at the Academy of 1790. In some ways this was the testing piece of his career. It did not attract unusual notice at the exhibition, but it gave him at the age of twenty-one an exceptional status. He was now the most promising portrait painter of the young generation and no longer a nine days' wonder. The paint throughout is controlled and vibrant—unlike *Lady Cremorne*—and the colour, in contrast to many of his portraits in this decade, is muted. At this exhibition it was not, however, *Queen Charlotte* but *Miss Farren* (Plate 3) which caught the popular imagination, and gave the first real indication of the type of portrait Lawrence was to introduce. *Miss Farren* was hung on the same wall as Reynolds's *Mrs. Billington as St. Cecilia* and the two

---

[1] *Whitehall Evening Post*, 15th May 1787.
[2] *The Hamwood Papers of the Ladies of Llangollen and Caroline Hamilton*, [Ed. Mrs. G. H. Bell], 1930, 80.
[3] Williams, II, 304.

pictures, by their very proximity, demanded comparison. Reynolds was in his sixty-eighth year and this was to prove the last time he exhibited. Lawrence was realizing his first success. *Mrs. Billington* is translated from the boards of Covent Garden to the skies with an academic gesture, *Miss Farren* from Drury Lane to open country with an easy but unacademic sophistication. In *Mrs. Billington* the Actress is metamorphosed to a Saint. In *Miss Farren* she is arch, inviting, and equivocal, more a woman than when on the stage. Correspondingly the paint of Lawrence is waxy, crisp and scintillating where the paint of Reynolds is creamy, churned and soft. The vivacity of *Miss Farren* augured extraordinary powers of development, and Sir Joshua contemplating the two portraits is reported to have made the magnanimous remark to Lawrence, 'In you, sir, the world will expect to see accomplished what I have failed to achieve.'

King George, who did not wholly approve the portrait of Queen Charlotte none the less admired Lawrence and wished to promote him. In 1790 when an Associateship of the Royal Academy was vacant he indicated, through the President, that he wished Lawrence to be elected. The message was resented by the academicians as interference and Lawrence was heavily outvoted in favour of Wheatley. He was, however, elected, an Associate in the following year, 1791.

On 23rd February 1792 Sir Joshua Reynolds died. Lawrence was at once offered the post of Painter in Ordinary to the King which Reynolds had held. He was also appointed to succeed him as Painter to the Dilettanti Society, and to make this possible a primary rule of the Society that 'no person was admissable as a member who had not crossed the Alps' was waived. Lawrence, as it proved, did not cross the channel, let alone the Alps, for another twenty-two years.

He was elected a Royal Academician in 1794, in his twenty-fifth year, when he defeated Hoppner, who was eleven years his senior, by two votes. The defeat, not unnaturally, was resented by Hoppner, and the rivalry between the two painters, insofar as it existed, was fostered by him rather than by Lawrence. Hoppner had at this time the favour of the Prince of Wales while Lawrence had the favour of the King, a circumstance which *de facto* placed them, in public opinion, in opposite camps, but which did not at any time affect the flow of commissions to either. It was, however, apparent soon after the death of Reynolds that at future exhibitions the critics would pit Hoppner and Lawrence against each other. The implications are so clearly stated by a writer in *The Monthly Mirror* for May 1796 that, although he comes down heavily on the side of Beechey against both the others, it is worth quoting him at length : 'A man of common sense and proportionate taste would be able at once to decide, without the assistance of any artificial jargon, of the portraits of Lawrence, Hoppner and Beechey which are the best: nor would the information that the two former were Royal Academicians and the latter but an associate bias his sentiments from their object; for Beechey has fewer eccentricities than his competitors—he never distorts his figure for the sake of extravagant attitude—he is less fantastic in his design and less exuberant in manner; in short he has more nature than the other two. Lawrence delights to be brilliant and Hoppner to be fine; one loses himself in gloss, the other in drapery. Beechey who is more fixed and determinate both in his colouring and outline studies only to be chaste.' The accusations of eccentricity and extravagance were aimed more at Lawrence than at Hoppner whose essays in full-length bravura were often unspeakably clumsy. He was a dogged painter with a gift for bold male character heads, but beside the glitter of a Lawrence his painting was dull. Throughout the 1790's he produced nothing to compare with the succession of full-length excitements that began with *Miss Farren* and ended in 1798 with *Lord Seaforth* (Plate 34). These included *Mr. and Mrs. Angerstein* (1792) (Plate 13), *Lord Mountstuart* (1794) (Plate 33), and *Miss Sarah Moulton Barrett* (1795) (Plate 31), and any estimate of the contribution of Lawrence to the development of English portraiture must derive in the first place from an assessment of this series. As inventions they are in the Reynolds tradition. *Lord Mountstuart* adopts, almost exactly, the pose of *Colonel St. Leger* in reverse. *Miss Moulton Barrett* takes on the stride of *Diana Viscountess Crosbie*. The allure of *Miss Farren* is, in origin, an enlivening of Reynolds's coy adaptations from Correggio. There is perhaps little new about the composition of these portraits, but there is a good deal that is new in their unscholarly exuberance, in the sparkle and bounce of a *Miss Barrett* which beside a Reynolds—even so unrestrained a Reynolds as *Miss Emily Pott as Thais*—has a suggestion of ill-breeding or at least of over-assurance. He achieves an illusion whereby the sitter seems to be advancing out of the picture, while the background recedes to infinity. In effect, the spectator views the scene from the circle. The stage becomes a panorama, and the rolling moors or parkland appear to extend below and behind the single actor endlessly. In almost all the portraits of Gainsborough and Reynolds the eye-level is lower, the horizon bounded, the movement slower. Lawrence in thus exaggerating the impact of the subject on the spectator sacrificed, for the time being, both the elegance of Gainsborough and the nobility of Reynolds. The contrast is perhaps emphasized today by the fact that the paint of a Lawrence has retained its freshness while the paint of a Reynolds has darkened and cracked, but there was no doubt justification for Anthony Pasquin's squibs on the exhibition of 1794 that the eyeballs of *Lord Auckland* seemed to be bursting from their spheres, and that *Richard Payne Knight* (Plate 29) had the appearance of an irascible pedagogue explaining Euclid to a dunce. In the quiet company of Hoppner, Beechey, Northcote, Owen and Shee the bravura of Lawrence could not but seem excessive.

Richard Payne Knight and *Georgiana Lady Apsley* (Plate 10), among the masterpieces of his early years, exhibit between them his qualities and his defects, on the one hand liveliness bordering on the theatrical, on the other charm bordering on the sentimental. They speak for all the portraits of the decade with the exception of *Lord Mountstuart*. Lord John, posed on the sierra in the costume of a Spanish Grandee, with storm clouds lowering behind him over the Escorial, is the first Byronic hero of English portraiture. This portrait arouses hopes of Lawrence developing as a romantic, some kind of English Delacroix, which are, unhappily, not fulfilled in the representations of John Philip Kemble playing heroic theatrical roles which he painted a few years later.

From his early days in London Lawrence made good friends in influential circles. Introductions by way of the Locks of Norbury to the Angersteins, the Allnutts, and the Boucherettes, opened many houses to him, and in these comfortable banking circles he found, as time went by, his natural companions. But of all his friends the closest was Joseph Farington the painter and Librarian to the Royal Academy. Farington gave him sound advice of every kind—on his painting, on professional etiquette, on the state of his finances, and on his most intimate affairs. Lawrence confided in him as he did in no-one else. The letters and notes that passed between them have been preserved in some number, and the references to Lawrence in Farington's Diary are exceedingly numerous. These reveal that essentially Lawrence was a temperamental man, dependent on the advice and affection of a few friends and by no means the suave courtier which later, in Society, he appeared to be. For the nineties the Diary has especial value, in that it records a number of criticisms of Lawrence's exhibited pictures and contains in Farington's own comments the views of a sensible and unemotional friend. In general Farington supported the critics. Lawrence was attacked chiefly on the one point of his extravagant use of high-lights, which, while they gave glitter or 'point' to his pictures, or parts of his pictures, cheapened them, and proved on examination to bear little or no relation to nature. He was also attacked for an excessive use of red in the shadows and of pink in the draperies. The extreme view was put by Fuseli, that 'when Lawrence distinguishes flesh from glass he will be a good artist'[1] and by Opie who remarked that his pictures had a 'tortoiseshell appearance'.[2] Lawrence himself, as late as 1798, admitted to Farington that he was sensible that his pictures 'had too much of a metallic appearance—too many shining lights'.[3] By the indiscriminate scattering of highlights he sometimes appeared to be dis-tracting the eye from deficiencies of drawing by a shop-window glitter. In this he gave a false impression. We know from his unfinished canvases and from the accounts of Farington and others that he drew the outline of the face and figure in some detail and with great care on the canvas before he began to paint. When he came to use the brush he seems to have been unable to resist weakening the structure of the figure by exaggera-tions. The explanation lay in that theatrical element in his nature which he no doubt inherited from his father who first exploited it at Devizes. Constantly praised for achieve-ments beyond his years, accepted before he was twenty as an equal in circles far above his own, summoned to paint the Queen at twenty-one, a full Academician at twenty-five: all these were circumstances to encourage this trait and to create in him a sense of unreality and of the spectacular.

He had always been attracted to the company of members of the theatrical world. At Bath he had twice made drawings of Mrs. Siddons, and the acquaintance was renewed in London where from the beginning he was an intimate of the Siddons-Kemble circle. The Theatre provided his favourite entertainment. Reading aloud was his favourite relaxation. He excelled in private theatricals and played before the Prince of Wales at one of the Marquess of Abercorn's parties at Stanmore Priory. It was of this occasion that Sheridan remarked that Lawrence was 'really *a very good actor*'. He was perhaps an actor in paint, and his ambitions as a painter, his successes and his limitations are all to some extent explained by a habit of mind based on a sense of theatre. While he remained a modest and unselfish man he was constantly concerned with the opinion of other people about himself, and his letters as they reveal his private life are essays in dramatization. They help to account for much that is contradictory in his production and behaviour in the years at the turn of the century.

LAWRENCE AND THE GRAND STYLE

Lawrence's devotion to the example of Sir Joshua's painting was extended to the *Discourses*. He believed that it should be the ambition of every painter to achieve the

[1] *The Farington Diary* [Ed. J. Grieg, 1923], 15th December 1796.
[2] *Ibid.*, 4th January 1797.   [3] *Ibid.*, 22nd July 1798.

Grand Style, and it was his misfortune that while undoubtedly he had the talent, he had not, through lack of training and of travel, the perception to achieve the kind of History picture he surmised. In *Satan* and the portraits of Kemble he convinced himself, but no-one else, that he was working towards 'the highest effort of the art'.

He once recorded that 'when a boy of fourteen or fifteen at Bath, Night after Night, and from Weeks to Months . . . I copied the Figures and Details from the Prophets and Sybils',[1] and in a letter from Bath to Dr. Falconer at Chester in 1785 he expounds at length on a drawing of Moses 'which does not come up to the conception I have . . . The figure must owe great part of its dignity to the size which must give it a fine effect'.[2] Clearly, from the first, grandeur was allied in his mind with size. His eight-foot canvas of *Christ Bearing the Cross* has disappeared. So too has the *Prospero Raising the Storm* which he exhibited in 1793—he later used this canvas for *J. P. Kemble as Rolla*—and the earliest surviving history piece, *Homer Reciting His Poems* (Plate 19) exhibited in 1791, is of small dimensions. This picture, which was painted for Richard Payne Knight, and still hangs at Downton Castle, succeeds as a pastiche of *The School of Athens* in the eighteenth-century taste, but hardly as an essay in the Raphaelesque. It is close in style to the work of his friend Westall with whom for a time he shared lodgings, and a number of whose works hang at Downton with it, and in no way does it foreshadow the greatest and last effort in his Grand Style, the *Satan Calling His Legions* (Plate 35) painted six years later in 1797. To the end of his life Lawrence believed that in *Satan*, and only in *Satan*, he had justified his reputation. When thirteen years later he went with Lord Mountjoy to see the picture again he 'return'd most heavily Depress'd in spirit from the strong impression of the past dreadful waste of time and improvidence of my life and talent . . . I have seen my own Picture with the Eye of a Spectator—of a Stranger—and I do know that it is such as neither Mr. West, nor Sir Joshua, nor Fuseli could have painted'.[3] The truth of the last observation carries, alas, no weight now, but at the time *Satan* was, for the most part, well received. With the exception of Pasquin the critics admired it. Today, bituminous and cracking, it commands respect as a conscientious failure.[4] Though it is conceivable that cleaning might bring back power to the head and life to the stagy flicker of Hellflames over the vast limbs it remains *une affaire manquée*, reminiscent not so much of Michelangelo as of Flaxman's recently published *Classical Outlines*. The obsession with size had achieved inflation but not grandeur.

Lawrence's rooms in Greek St. were beginning to fill with plaster casts from the antique, and in so far as he alluded to classical prototypes in his portraits—the *Venus de' Medici* in *Miss Jennings*, the *Diane Chasseresse* in *Lady Conyngham* (Plate 50)—he was making use of studio properties. In attempting Michelangelesque subjects on a Michelangelesque scale as in *Satan* Lawrence was of his age in the company of Haydon, but in carrying this scale into portraiture he was alone. Benjamin West was one of the few who perceived this, and he observed with reference to the female portraits of this date, 'The Greek made his Apollo Colossal, but his Venus a little figure. Lawrence aims at the antique in forming his style but has not perceived this error.'[5]

[1] G. S. Layard, *Sir Thomas Lawrence's Letter-Bag*, 1906, 169.
[2] In the City of Bath Reference Library.   [3] Layard, 84.
[4] The Royal Academy hoped that cleaning and, possibly, discreet restoration might be possible, but careful examination indicates that nothing had better be attempted.
[5] Farington [unpublished] 15th March 1801.

Satan was followed in 1798 by *John Philip Kemble as Coriolanus* (Plate 36) the first of three gigantic apotheoses of this actor. *Kemble as Rolla* was exhibited in 1800 and *Kemble as Hamlet* (Plate 49) in 1801. Here in scenes of theatrical eloquence demanding an eloquent inflationary style, Lawrence invented a compromise with the grand Italian manner in a grand Theatrical manner which was suited to his capabilities. He admitted the compromise when he called the Kemble portraits 'half-history' pictures. It was an invention that did not admit of great variations. The Kemble portraits are all very much alike— the spotlit figure, the heroic stance, the commanding eye—and it is perhaps as well that only one more appeared in the series, the *Kemble as Cato* of 1812. Lawrence spoke of Reynolds' *Mrs. Siddons as the Tragic Muse* as the finest female portrait in the world, and in these portraits of her brother he no doubt constantly measured himself against it. Despite his good opinion of them and the polite esteem with which they were accepted, he found it difficult to dispose of prestige-pictures of this kind. Only one, *Coriolanus*, found an early purchaser, Sir Richard Worsley. *Satan*, which was eventually bought by the Duke of Norfolk, came back to Lawrence after the Duke's death in 1815 and remained on his hands until he died. *Rolla*, despite the fact that Lord Whitworth proposed to take it with him to Paris as a showpiece for the British Embassy,[1] was unsold until 1827 when it was bought by Sir Robert Peel. It last appeared in the Peel Heirlooms sale in 1900. *Cato*, which was commissioned by Lord Mountjoy, later Earl of Blessington, seems to have remained in Lawrence's studio and was not delivered until 1831. This also has disappeared. Most extraordinary is the history of *Hamlet*. Some time between its first exhibition in 1801 and its sale by public auction in 1812 it was purchased by a Mr. Maddocks M.P., who had the fantastic intention of setting it up as an altarpiece in the church he had newly built in the village of Tre Madoc in Wales. The Bishop of the diocese objected, and it was sent for sale to London when it was bought by one Robert Ashby who sold it back to Lawrence.[2] A few years later the Duke of Abercorn planned to buy it to hang in the saloon at Stanmore but he died before the purchase was completed. It was sold at last to George IV; and finally, in 1836, William IV presented it to the nation.

The Kemble portraits were the last of the ambitious efforts. The Duke of Norfolk's proposed commission for a *Granting of the Magna Carta to the Barons*, twenty-five feet high, for Arundel Castle never, fortunately, materialized, for Lawrence almost certainly would have accepted it. His mind, however, continued to run on this kind of project and he planned a *Building of the Parthenon* which could only have been worked out to large dimensions. He describes it in an undated letter to Mrs. Wolff, 'Pericles! Pericles! Pericles! Let all your thoughts dear Adviser be on him, for determined upon it I am. And now think of Aspasia, Anaxagoras, Damon, Socrates, Alcibiades, Phidias. What think you of their being placed under the magnificent portico when building? which gives me in the varied action of workmen etc. on ladders, lifting immense weights, every display of the naked figure, which others cannot achieve and I can—their forms now bright against the deep blue of the sky, and now as shadows against its lighter hues, contrasted with the solemn magnificence of the group below. I think we must give Alcibiades his flowing hair, his indolent graceful manner, and the long trailing of his robe.'[3]

Sir George Beaumont made the shrewd remark at about the time of the exhibition of *Satan* that Lawrence 'had been induced by ambition to attempt subjects out of the natural

---

[1] Farington, 24th February 1803.   [2] *Art Union*, August 1841.   [3] Williams, II, 65.

choice of his mind which would lead him to Guido rather than to Michelangelo'.[1] According-ing to Lawrence's own avowal such subjects *were* the natural choice of his mind, but on the evidence of his portraits and drawings it is clear that his bent was for the romantic rather than the sublime. Romantic landscape excited his imagination. The history picture inhibited it. 'You have touched a weakness in me', he once wrote, 'in mentioning a land-scape, for the survey of Nature has always been enjoyment to me and I have always felt that I had some power in representing it.'[2] Some of the best passages of painting in his early portraits—that is before about 1803 after which the backgrounds become more sketchy and are largely the work of assistants—are the landscapes: the view of Eton College in *Queen Charlotte*, the sierra in *Lord Mountstuart*—and the most attractive of his draw-ings are studies of park and woodland in chalk on grey paper. There is also at least one pen and ink sketch of flowers with detailed colour notes of petal and leaf.[3] Several small landscape studies in oil survive and two (Plates 20, 21) were engraved shortly after his death.

To call Lawrence a Romantic would be to link him falsely with the generation that followed his own. He belonged to the eighteenth century. His aspirations never wavered from the *Discourses*, though perhaps he never fully understood them. The Romantic as Professor Mario Praz defines him, 'The poet ecstatic in front of the forever blank page', would not have been sympathetic to him. There was, none the less, a good deal of the restless melancholic in his make-up. He complained of 'constitutional languor'. His notes to Farington echo with frantic appeals, 'For God's sake call on me as soon as you can'. As his debts increased his correspondence with his bankers ran to sixteen page letters of justification and desperation. He was handsome. His love affairs, as far as they were affairs, and if he really was in love, were much discussed, and it was in keeping with his temperament and his career that his name was one of those linked, groundlessly, with that of the Princess of Wales in the scandals which led to the Delicate Investigation of 1806. His one serious entanglement, the business of broken engagements with Sally and Maria Siddons, was carried through in hectic terms. The Passions played their full part in his self-dramatization, and in a revealing letter to Thomas Coutts written when his affairs were desperate he compared himself dejectedly to the prosperous business-like Reynolds but added with something like pride that Sir Joshua was 'of a cold Temperament, a philosopher from absence of the Passions'.[4] This was the Lawrence who wrote, 'I would rather paint Satan bursting into tears, when collecting his ruined angels, than Achilles, radiant in his heavenly arms, mounting his chariot, defying his destiny when announced by miracle, and rushing on devoted Troy! And fallen Rome, with its declining sun, as it was once sweetly, pathetically painted by Claude, would be more delightful in anticipation than seen in its full carnival, with its rich tapestries hung round St. Peter's, its illuminated dome and the magnificent fireworks from the castle of St. Angelo.'[5]

1800–1805

Lawrence's financial difficulties grew with his reputation and practice. In 1793 he had fixed his price at 40 guineas for a head and shoulders, 80 guineas for a half-length and

---

[1] Farington [unpublished], 7th April 1797.
[2] In a letter to Sir Robert Peel, 7th March 1825, now in the Library of the Fitzwilliam Museum, Cambridge.
[3] In the collection of Mr. Iolo Williams.　[4] From a letter in the archives of Coutts Bank.　[5] Williams, II, 49.

160 guineas for a whole-length. At this time he was paying a rental of 200 guineas for rooms in Bond Street, and allowing £300 a year to his father. In 1794 he moved to a house in Piccadilly at a rental of £250 and spent about £500 in making improvements over the next three years. In 1797 his father died but he seems to have continued to some extent to support his sisters. He was living all this time well beyond his means, although in addition to the income from portrait commissions which must have been ample, he received about £500 a year in his capacity as Painter in Ordinary to the King for repetitions of Sir Joshua's royal portraits. His dread of a failure to keep up appearances provoked him to constant overspending and constant borrowing, and despite loans from sitters, advice from Farington, and extreme forbearance by his banker, Thomas Coutts, he was by 1800 in a hopeless position. In 1801 there were said to be thirty actions pending against him. Coutts advised a declaration of bankruptcy but this he managed to avoid by procrastination, pleading, further borrowing, and a plan of economical living which he only partially observed. These were the years of his entanglement with the Siddons daughters. It is not therefore surprising that between 1797 and 1806 the quality of his work was more than usually uneven. He accepted far more commissions than he could execute, profiting by his rule that half the purchase price should be paid at the first sitting; and he worked ceaselessly . . . 'I have now Four and Five sitters in a Day and have no choice without absolutely affronting them between receiving them and finishing other Pictures . . . The close of the Day has found me tir'd and exhausted and produc'd its consequent languor of the Mind.'[1] Tiredness is evident in many of the portraits of this date.

He had employed pupil assistants as early as 1793 when Thomas Hargreaves of Liverpool joined him for two years, and it is probable that he was never without them from this time. In the nineties they must have been employed chiefly on repetitions of royal portraits for the houses of government representatives abroad, but after 1800, if not before, they certainly had a hand in the portrait commissions. Samuel Lane who joined the studio in 1800 and remained with Lawrence for some years soon became his chief assistant. George Harlow signed a contract as a pupil assistant in 1802 and stayed about eighteen months. Lane certainly, and Harlow probably (though it must be noted that he was only sixteen at the time) painted a good part of the large number of rather slipshod head and shoulders portraits of women which came from Lawrence's studio between 1800 and 1806. They almost all follow the same pattern, full face, half left, the left elbow resting on a pillar, the forearm drooping, having, apparently, no connection to the rest of the body. The vitality of the early portraits had gone, and Lawrence's reputation began to suffer. In particular the full-length portrait of *Mrs. Siddons* exhibited in 1804 caused considerable disappointment. To be just to his mercurial temperament it must be remembered that he also produced within these years one of the most vivacious of his female heads, the *Hon. Emily Lamb* (Plate 54), and one of the finest of his male three-quarters, *Lord Thurlow* (Plate 51); and the truth must be weighed of Benjamin West's remark that 'Lawrence is one of those who as an artist would be ruined but for annual Exhibitions which recall his attention and would make him feel the necessity of Exertion'.[2]

[1] From a letter to Edward Antrobus, 10th May 1803, in the possession of Coutts Bank.
[2] Farington, 10th April 1804.

10

INTRODUCTION

1805–1814

Despite these personal embarrassments Lawrence was quoted in Academy circles as a likely successor to Benjamin West who resigned the Presidency in December 1805, but his name, at the time of election, was not put forward. The post went for one year to Wyatt, and West was re-elected in 1806.

Lawrence was now thirty-seven years of age and successfully established. He seems to have accepted the cautious advice of Farington, given two years earlier, 'to be satisfied at present & to endeavour to establish himself at the Head of that Department [portrait painting] by aiming at all possible excellence, and some years hence, after He shall have acquired fame & fortune, there will be full time, considering his age, only thirty-five to make any other effort'.[1]

The years 1806 to 1812 saw a consolidation and broadening of his powers. The affairs of the heart were over. He had come to an agreement with his bankers. He had abandoned the ambition to paint on a vast scale, and he concentrated instead on the problem of 'composing' within the limits of a portrait group. The nervous excitement of the early full-lengths gave place to deliberation, to the intellectual pursuit of 'those forms and lines which constitute beauty',[2] and a greater subtlety of colour. It was generally agreed that at the successive Academy exhibitions of 1806, 1807 and 1808, he excelled himself in the *Fancy Group* (Mrs. Maguire and Arthur Fitzjames, Plate 59), *Sir Francis Baring John Baring and Charles Wall* (Plate 60) and the posthumous portrait of *Pitt* (Plate 63). *Mrs. Maguire* and the *Baring* group rank with *Lady Grey and Children* (1805) and *Mrs. Henry Baring and Children* (1821) (Plate 92) as his most complicated essays in composition. In *Mrs. Maguire* (Farington's 'circular Picture') he attempted, not with complete success, to arrest the passing moment. The result is a slightly uncomfortable spread-eagling. He returned to variations on the same centrally pivoted pattern in *Mrs. Stratton* (1812) (Plate 70) and *Miss Julia Peel* (1826) (Plate 103). These new portrait groups were by no means his first. In the nineties he painted at least six, of which four were on a full-length scale, but his concern at that time was immediacy rather than composing. The *Cavendish Children* (Plate 15) tumble out of their portrait restrained by no controlling design. The effect is charming and less artificial than the arrested motion of *Mrs. Maguire* but the picture is conceived on a lower intellectual plane. On the other hand the *Sons of Lord Talbot* (Plate 14), the most important of the early groups, unites a noble design with the elegance one expects to find in a large scale pastel portrait by John Russell.

In the Baring group Lawrence created a drama. This portrait was commissioned by Sir Francis Baring as a companion to the Reynolds group of his political associates *Lord Ashburton, Colonel Barré, and the Marquess of Lansdowne.* Beside the dignified immobility of the Reynolds the Lawrence is tense. The Barings are actors, Lord Ashburton and his friends spectators. In this respect it is so successful that it raises the problem—as Lawrence portraits do from time to time throughout his career—of how successful he might, after all, have proved in history painting had his talent been allowed a slow and natural development. Lawrence possessed considerable mental qualities which the forcing house atmosphere of Devizes and Bath must have somewhat stunted.

---

[1] Farington, 8th September 1804.
[2] In a letter from Lawrence to J. W. Croker, 8th July 1829 *of The Croker Papers* [ed. Jennings], 1884.

INTRODUCTION

He received for the *Baring* group 300 guineas, and in this year, 1807, he raised his charges for the first time since 1793. They now stood at 50 guineas for a head and shoulders, 70 guineas for a Kitcat, 100 guineas for a half-length, 120 guineas for a bishop's half-length, 200 guineas for a whole length. These approximate to the charges made by Reynolds at the time of his death.

In 1810 Hoppner died. Lawrence had now no rival and on 27th April 1811, on the occasion of the Royal Academy banquet, Farington was able to record in his diary: "Lawrence whose professional fame was this day established by the general acknowledgment of the superior excellence of his works, came home with me and had tea.' In May he raised his prices to a scale rising to 300 guineas for a whole length.

1814–1818

In April 1814, when the Emperor of Russia and the King of Prussia were expected on a visit to England, Lady Anne Barnard, the authoress of *Auld Robin Grey*, wrote to the Regent proposing a portrait group of himself and the two monarchs to commemorate the allied victory over Napoleon. The Prince was flattered and the name of Lawrence was suggested as the painter. Lady Anne wrote to Lawrence explaining her proposal in detail. By this time she envisaged two pictures 'of very considerable size'; one to represent Louis XVIII taking from his shoulders the Order of St. Esprit and throwing it over the shoulders of the Regent with the words, 'To you Sir I have owed my all!—even my sustenance—I have nothing to give you but THIS—keep it to remind you of Louis XVIII'[1] —with, as an afterthought, the Duchesse D'Angoulême fitted in to 'add interest and charm'; the second to be a group of the Emperors of Austria and Russia and the King of Prussia with their victorious generals, the Princess Charlotte looking on 'for interest and charm' and Lawrence himself as an attendant figure.

Two months later Lord Charles Stewart, the newly appointed Ambassador to Austria, proposed that Lawrence should go out with him to Vienna at the time fixed for the Congress and paint the Emperors there. This practical suggestion took precedence over Lady Anne's flight of fancy.

It was decided that Lawrence should go to Vienna in January 1815 as the envoy of the Regent to paint the heads of the allied states and armies, and that to give him greater status abroad he should be knighted. He received his knighthood, but the plan of travel was frustrated by the flight of Napoleon from Elba and the Hundred Days. He had already painted Prince Blucher, the Hetman Platoff, Prince Metternich and the Duke of Wellington at his studio in Russell Square, and had made sketches at St. James's Palace of the Emperor Alexander and King Frederick. In this manner was begun the great series of portraits which hang now in the Waterloo Chamber built to receive them at Windsor Castle.

1818–1820

The Vienna plan hung fire for three years. Lawrence set out finally for Aix-la-Chapelle, the first stage of his journey, on 29th September 1818. His terms were £500 for each full-length portrait with £1,000 for travelling and out-of-pocket expenses. This as far as records

[1] A. Aspinall, *The Letters of King George IV*, Cambridge, 1938, I, 438.

12

show was only his second visit abroad. He had crossed the channel for the first time in 1815 when he went over to Paris for two or three weeks to see the exhibition of works of art looted by Napoleon during his campaigns. Lawrence strongly advocated the permanent retention of the whole collection in France. There is a touching story that as he stood in a courtyard of the Louvre with Chantrey and Canova, the *Venus de' Medici* was trundled out to a waiting wagon on its way back to Italy. As it passed the three artists they burst into tears with one accord.[1]

A prefabricated studio erected at government expense should have been shipped in time to await his arrival at Aix. It was delayed and he was allotted a painting-room in the Hôtel de Ville which he declared 'the best I ever had'. Here he received further sittings from both Emperors and the King of Prussia and almost completed their portraits. Lawrence left for Vienna early in December, and the five months he spent there away from the usual press of sitters and from his creditors, must have given him more security and more leisure than he had enjoyed for many years. As the Regent's Envoy and the guest of Lord Charles Stewart, who counted him as a friend, he was received by the Metternichs and introduced to the 'first circle' of Viennese society. He worked hard completing the portrait of the Emperor and painting, in addition, three large whole-lengths and one small, three half-lengths, five heads and the small portrait of the infant *Princess Maria Theresia* (Plate 83). He also made about a dozen portrait drawings and an oil sketch of the son of Napoleon. A sense of the importance of his 'mission'—the word occurs constantly in his letters—gave a new authority to his portraiture. The complete assurance of pose and placing of the *Archduke Charles* (Plate 88), the apparently nonchalant but perfect balance between flamboyance and restraint, are achieved with an *haut ton* as far removed from the scholarly British vigour of Reynolds's *Colonel Tarleton* as from Sargent's or Orpen's journalists' character sketches of the leaders of the 1914–18 war. Moreover, while in Vienna he paid long visits to Imperial and private collections, enriching his knowledge of Rubens and Titian, and discovering Velazquez for the first time. Certainly the remembrance of the portraits of the Infantas was strong seven years later when he painted *Lady Robert Manners* (Plate 113) in which the dominant colour is blue.

While he was at Aix Lawrence received instructions from London to extend his tour to Rome to paint the Pope and Cardinal Consalvi. He was now fifty years of age and this was his first visit to Italy. He arrived in Rome on 10th May 1819 intending to complete his work and return to England quickly, but he stayed until 22nd December. In these seven months he painted only the two portraits, as if in the repose of the Roman scene he found some respite for the restlessness of forty years, some time for relaxation which his career as a prodigy and his temperament had, until now, denied him. He spent hours in the Sistine Chapel, and the Stanze of the Vatican, but he employed other men to make copies for him. More surprisingly it does not appear that he made many sketches on his walks in the city or his excursions to the Campagna or to Tivoli. One oil sketch, a *View on the Tiber*, was included in the sale of his collections at Christie's on 17th June 1830, and has since disappeared.

Lawrence was now accepted as the first portrait painter of Europe and as a distinguished member of the cosmopolitan society that moved in the European capitals. The Metternichs

[1] Dorothy M. Quynn, *The Art Confiscations of the Napoleonic Wars* in *The American Historical Review*, April 1925.

and the Duchess of Devonshire were spending the summer in Rome and he spent much of his time in their company, or in that of the Torlonias. In their carriages he drove about the environs of the city. When he could he would go in the early evening to the Villa Pamphili and look down on the panorama in the fading light. Such occasions moved him profoundly . . . 'I have this evening driven there alone (having determined to be to myself this whole day) and felt the exceeding beauty of the scene with that undefined loneliness of delight which amounts almost to pain, formed, as it is, of many causes—thoughts of the past—of youth—of friends and absence, which I think, when alone, the close of evening in the country always brings before us.'[1]

In Rome Lawrence admitted the public to his painting room. They could see there the Vienna portraits and the *J. J. Angerstein* (Plate 75) which had travelled with him from London. The completed portraits of the Pope and the Cardinal were exhibited before he left the city, and so, three years later was the portrait of King George IV in garter robes which the Pope had commissioned. All these caused something of a sensation. In contrast to the emasculated neo-classicism of Vincenzo Camuccini, the foremost painter of Rome, the Lawrence portraits were startling. The flow of his brush won him the title of 'Il Tiziano Inglese'. Among many comments one that is amusing and also illuminating comes in a letter from Dorothea Schlegel to her brother Friedrich on 19th June 1819, 'Even the mice will enjoy a picture like this as there is at least ten pounds of oil paint smeared all over it.'[2]

On the journey from Rome to London Lawrence stayed nearly three months in Florence. He arrived in England on 20th March 1820. On 10th March Benjamin West had died and Lawrence was elected to succeed him as President of the Royal Academy by an almost unanimous vote.

1820–1825

It has sometimes been stated that in the last ten years of his life Lawrence pandered to the taste of the readers of *The Keepsake*, *The Bijou*, and *The Amulet*. This is only true in the sense that the more modish portraits of society women he exhibited at this time were sentimentalized in the engravings which appeared in those knick-knack annuals, and that the originals have been blamed for the faults of the engravings. When Haydon said that 'Lawrence was suited to the age and the age to Lawrence', suggesting a surrender to meretricious taste, he was right in that Lawrence adapted his style to the mood of the day, but wrong in the implication that he lowered his professional standards. *The Countess of Blessington* (Plate 96), *Lady Georgiana Agar-Ellis and Son* (Plate 102) and *Lady Wallscourt* (Plate 97) are highly artificial creations—in Fuseli's phrase 'an attempt of uniting the Goddess with the Belle'[3]—and no doubt exactly fulfilled the sitter's estimation of her own appearance. To Lawrence, however, having at last a first hand knowledge of the galleries of Europe, they were in the first place further developments of those essays in composing which began with *Mrs. Maguire and Arthur Fitzjames*. The line is yet more flowing, the paint more fluid, the colour more refined. The presence of ermine and strawberry leaf is

[1] Williams, II, 183.
[2] The German text is quoted in Gerstenberg and Rave, *Die Wandgemälde der Deutscher Romantiker im Casa Massimo in Rom*, Berlin, 1934. I am indebted to Dr. Leopold Ettlinger for this reference.
[3] From a manuscript notice of the R.A. exhibition, 1803, in private possession.

yet more subtly indicated. To this extent perhaps the diner-out cajoles the academician but he never over-rules him. The elongation of neck and arm, the gloss of ringlet and bosom and bracelet, are another phase in the arrangement of 'those forms and lines which constitute beauty', almost creating a Regency or late Georgian Mannerist period in English portrait painting.

The highly skilful *Calmady Children* (Plate 99) and *Master Lambton* (Plate 98) touch the artificial more dangerously. What had been high spirits thirty years earlier in *Harriet and Emily Lamb* (Plate 11) has here become sentimental idealization—the 'Guido' strain diagnosed in 1797 by Beaumont. The change perhaps was less in Lawrence himself than in the times, the difference between the elegant yet sensible appointments of a drawing-room of nineties and the bric-à-brac which figured so largely in the sale of Lady Blessington's effects at Gore House. He was it seems one of those men who respond instinctively and unconsciously to the tone and the taste of the day, and who while steadfastly proclaiming the highest standards of their creed, are by subtle influences sometimes led to betray them. In the case of *Master Lambton* and the *Calmady Children* there is evidence of a relaxing of effort, of an easy exercise of charm, which no longer has its roots in the eighteenth century, but is itself one of the roots of mid-nineteenth century academic speciousness. Both pictures had an immediate success in France where engravings of them sold in large numbers. Contrary to the statements of Williams and others, neither was shown at the Salon—unless they were added to the exhibitions after the catalogues were printed—but it seems certain that they were both exhibited somewhere in Paris soon after they were painted, and that they were extremely popular. Burger seeing *Master Lambton* for the first time at the Manchester Art Treasures Exhibition in 1857 wrote with some disappointment 'le fameux *Master Lambton* . . . n'a pas toutes les qualités qu'on croyait y voir lorsqu'il eut tant de succès à Paris en 1824'. The Salon Catalogue of 1824 does, however, contain one Lawrence portrait, a *Duc de Richelieu*, no doubt the version now in the Waterloo Chamber at Windsor. This was acclaimed by the young painters of the French Romantic Movement, along with the works exhibited by Constable, Bonington and the Copley Fieldings, as achieving a naturalism, a freedom from convention and, in the case of Constable, a brilliance of colour, which seemed to epitomize their aspirations at the time. The immediate reaction of Delacroix, who visited Lawrence in London in 1825, is clear in the portrait of Baron Schwiter, painted in 1826, and now in the National Gallery. He patently follows the example of Lawrence in isolating the single figure on a terrace against a looming expanse of sky, and he restricts his palette to a Lawrence key.

The year 1825 was the occasion of Lawrence's third visit to France and last visit abroad, when he was sent by the King to Paris to paint the portraits of Charles X and the Dauphin. These were among his last official commissions, and they complete the Waterloo Chamber series. His personal success with the King and the Dauphin was as great as it had been in Rome with the Pope, and in Vienna with the Metternichs. He was persuaded to paint a portrait of the *Duchesse de Berri* (Plate 100), and he returned to England an officer of the Legion of Honour, bringing with him presents from the King of a dessert service of Sèvres porcelain and from the Dauphin of a breakfast set 'in a green leather and gold bordered box'. These are mentioned in the impressive list of gifts 'from foreign princes' drawn up by his sister for the information of Williams which also included 'the Colosseum in Mosaic' from the Pope, and 'a superb diamond ring of great value' from the Emperor of Russia.

INTRODUCTION

1825–1830

In the last years of his life Lawrence achieved some of his finest and most penetrating work. He was now an honorary member of most of the Academies of Europe and of the American Academy of Fine Arts, and the esteem in which he was held abroad, the continuing favour of the King, and his successful administration as President of the Royal Academy all helped to give him greater security. The misgivings he expressed so frequently, earlier in life, ceased to trouble him. He was always inclined to an optimistic conviction that a portrait he had just finished was better than any he had done before, but it is most certainly true that he never painted a lady of fashion better than *Lady Peel* (Plate 101), or the head of a profession better than *John Nash* (Plate 108) or a shrewd and contented old lady better than *Mrs. Lock* (Plate 111). In *Lady Peel* he transformed the vulgarity of plumes, satins, furs, and ostentatious jewellery into a portrait not altogether unworthy to hang, as this was intended, as a pendant to the Rubens '*Chapeau de Paille*' which then formed part of Sir Robert Peel's collection. From his first introduction to the *Lion Hunt* at Corsham in the 1770's he had expressed an unvarying devotion to Rubens. The Baring group and the full length portraits in the Waterloo Chamber derive from him; but never before had he placed so direct a challenge as this.

John Nash and *Mrs. Lock* serve as well as any of the later portraits as a basis for an assessment of Lawrence's final style. He was always moved to his best work by an elderly sitter, and it is questionable if as character studies either of these portraits is more penetrating than *Lord Barrington* painted almost forty years earlier, but as portrait-compositions they have an air of distinction which the earlier picture lacks. In the twenties comments on Lawrence portraits abounded in the journals and the correspondence of the day. Thomas Campbell wrote that 'Lawrence's sitters seem to have got in a drawing room in the mansions of the blessed and to be looking at themselves in a mirror', and John Wilson Croker in a letter to John Murray à propos Moore's *Life of Byron* put the same kind of generalization with rather more discernment, 'Moore has done for him [Byron] what poor Lawrence has done for so many: enforced merits; softened defects; preserved a likeness; and made a fine picture'. These two comments express between them something very near the whole truth. Lawrence never conquered, perhaps never wished to conquer, the habit of looking at his sitter as at an actor on a stage. The sitter assumes a self-conscious air and too often there seems to be only an exchange of drawing-room courtesies between them; but in his best work while the courtesies are maintained the understanding is deepened. In Nash, a professional acquaintance of long standing, and Mrs. Lock, a friend for forty years, the charming hostess of Norbury Park until the death of her husband in 1810, he had sitters too well acquainted with him to allow any kind of portrait but the most direct and the most thoughtful. Other portraits of the same calibre belong to the same years, *Sir John Soane, Lady Skipwith*, and the unfinished *William Wilberforce* (Plate 119). There is every reason to think that had he lived ten years longer Lawrence might at the end of life have developed as a forcible painter of character. It is possible that his best work had yet to come.

Lawrence died unexpectedly from sudden ossification of the heart following a chill, on 7th January 1830, and was buried on 20th January with great honours in St. Paul's Cathedral. At the time of his death his price for a full-length portrait was 700 guineas. He was succeeded as President of the Royal Academy by Martin Archer Shee, and as Painter in Ordinary to the King by David Wilkie.

He left in the rooms of his house in Russell Square about two hundred unfinished portraits, a few of them dating as far back as the 1790's and a good many to before 1810. About one hundred and fifty were claimed by the sitters or their families who had long ceased to expect to see them finished. The remainder were included in the sales of his effects at Christie's in 1830 and 1831, and of these some could be identified. This means that there were not more than thirty or forty portraits to which a name could not be attached at the time. The haphazard attribution to Lawrence by dealers and collectors of almost any unidentified portrait head approximating to his style has been based on a vague belief that some hundreds of unfinished pictures came on the market from his studio after his death. This has led to an equally irresponsible scattering of celebrated names, and any 'unrecorded' portrait 'by Lawrence' of Mrs. Siddons, of Sally or Maria Siddons, of Canning, Castlereagh or Wellington—the names which most frequently occur—must be regarded with grave doubt. So must any 'Self-Portrait'. Lawrence made several drawings of himself as a young man, and one portrait in oils, and he painted a charming miniature self-portrait for a bracelet for Miss Croft,[1] but in later years he was extremely reluctant to attempt a self-portrait of any kind and only the unfinished picture at the Royal Academy can be accepted as authentic. Of this a number of copies and variants were made in the studio.

A good deal of confusion on the subject of the unfinished pictures can be avoided by reference to the extremely careful list, drawn up by Lawrence's executor, Archibald Keightley, of all the portraits claimed from the studio and of the degree to which they were 'finished' at the time. This list was acquired by the Victoria and Albert Museum in 1934 and the relevant entries are quoted as Appendix III to this book. At the request of the claimants a number of portraits were completed by studio assistants, of whom Richard Evans, John Simpson and Frederick Say were most frequently employed. Others were completed by Samuel Lane who was by this time working on his own. I have included in the catalogue all the portraits in this list even though in one or two cases Lawrence had done little more than sketch in the head. The portrait of the Marchioness of Waterford is, for instance, indicated by Keightley as only one-sixth finished.

The number of Lawrence's assistants at any one time and the extent of their work still remains a problem. It appears that from about the year 1800 he accepted 'pupils' who in return for a premium of one hundred guineas were allowed to make copies and to ask his advice. From these he would select the most able as pupil-assistants. He did not offer any systematic training, and was himself so busy that he rarely had time to give the advice his pupils had a right to ask. Lane, who was his chief assistant at intervals from about 1802, complained to Farington: 'I go on badly with Mr. Lawrence. He does not employ me in a regular way, and I lose much time in consequence of his being undetermined how to employ me . . . He sometimes walks about uncertain what to give me, & at last puts into my hand a three quarter portrait, desiring me to paint to it a *plain background* which I can do in three quarters, & I am then again witht. employ. Sometimes in a great hurry He puts pictures into my hands to be forwarded for finishing witht. delay.'[2] This was in 1806. In 1807 William Etty came as a 'pupil' and was given quarters in the house in Greek

---

[1] In the possession of Major O. G. S. Croft.   [2] Farington, 7th May 1806.

Street. He found that he scarcely ever saw Lawrence, and felt in later years that the hundred guineas his uncle had paid for him was a sum of money wasted. He did, however, in that year become extremely proficient at painting in the Lawrence manner. Two good copies, a head of Lady Templetown and a head of one of the Pattison Boys, are now in the Art Gallery at York. There must have been a number of other pupils coming and going for a year at a time and left very much to their own devices. Farington mentions one other Mr. Agar, a 'natural son of Lord Callan'; but for the most part their names are recorded only by chance in letters and memoirs. Lawrence himself makes little reference to pupils or assistants until in a letter to Angerstein written in November 1821 he makes it clear that he had by that time a rather more organized system and an over-full house: 'I have long been in want of a large room for pupils and assistants but the difficulty of finding one near me, and the inconvenience and probable loss attending the progress of their labours at any distance from me, have hitherto prevented my attaining this highly necessary object. From this difficulty I shall now be relieved by converting the attics of my house into one large room or possibly two: in which I can have one superior disciple [a phrase in the good old style] and in the largest room others who may be painting together. All will then be under my own eye and any progress be thus extended and quickened.'

The recognized extent of a pupil-assistant's work in a head and shoulders portrait is explained in a letter from Keightley to Admiral Sir Edward Codrington. Sir Edward had complained at having to pay the full price for a portrait completed by assistants. Keightley replies: 'You suggest that your picture has been in part painted by pupils and most probably you are right. Sir Thomas in common with all eminent artists in that branch of painting avowedly and invariably used the assistance of others in completing the minor parts of his pictures. The original design, the head and the sketching of the figure were his own, if a pupil performed any part of the rest it was no breach of contract but consistent with a known and necessary custom'.[1]

★ ★ ★

The death of Lawrence came as a shock to the nation for he had become a national figure to a degree achieved by no English portrait painter before him, Reynolds not excepted. This was due not only to the quality of his portraiture which far excelled that of his contemporaries and juniors in technical ability and invention. Nor was it a reputation based wholly on the exceptional publicity which Royal favour and the success of the European tour had given him. Despite his irresponsibility as a man of business and as a teacher, he was esteemed in the first place for his personal qualities. He was a man of integrity, of candour and consideration, of fine bearing and exceptional generosity, and of sound judgment in most matters outside the management of his own affairs. The collection of old master drawings, which partly accounted for his debts, was one of the finest ever made. His evidence in favour of the Elgin marbles carried considerable weight in the decision of the government to acquire them for the British Museum. He advised John Angerstein to offer his father's collection of pictures to the nation at a sum considerably less than he might have obtained from the Prince of Orange, and so helped indirectly to found the National Gallery of which he was one of the first Trustees. He gave constant help and encouragement to young artists. He designed the seal of the Athenaeum.

[1] From a letter dated 1st March 1830, in the possession of Col. G. R. Codrington.

In countless ways and in varied circles his advice was sought and acted upon, and probably no obituary notice touched the truth so nearly as the casual remark of his housekeeper, 'Poor Sir Thomas, always something to worrit him'. These worries were not always financial, but it should be recorded that the sale of his collection and effects which realized over £37,000 only just cancelled his debts. His heirs—that is his surviving sister Anne (Mrs. Bloxam), her children, and the daughter of his sister Lucy, (Mrs. Meredith)—received only the proceeds from the Memorial Exhibitions held at the British Institution in 1830 and 1833, and Mrs. Bloxam had to buy in from the executors even such personal items as his diplomas, his Cross of the Legion of Honour, his rings, his pencil cases, and his reading glass.

★   ★   ★

Benjamin Robert Haydon, who veered between intense admiration and extreme dislike of Lawrence, wrote one sentence about him which serves as well as any for his epitaph: 'Weakened and harassed as Lawrence was by the habits of society there were always gleams of power about him that made me lament that Nature did not quite finish his capacity.' He was very nearly a great painter. While it is true that the romantic side of his nature ran to sentiment, that his powers of invention needed the constant stimulus of exhibitions or historic events, that his mind while swift and adaptable was not highly original, he yet remains one of the most exciting of British portrait painters. He drew, and handled paint, with exceptional brilliance, and his work provides such constant hints of power latent but unexpressed that any assessment which belittles him leaves in the mind a serious doubt.

ACKNOWLEDGEMENTS

IN 1900 Algernon Graves published a comparatively short list of the 'exhibited and engraved works' of Lawrence which was printed as an appendix to Lord Ronald Sutherland Gower's *Sir Thomas Lawrence*. This was followed in 1913 by the considerably enlarged and more detailed catalogue compiled by Sir Walter Armstrong. Neither catalogue is by any means complete, and Armstrong is much less reliable than Graves; but before Graves no attempt to list the work of Lawrence had been made, and without these two books the task of beginning such a list today would be formidable indeed. Since 1913 a large amount of new material has become available. The Farington Diary has been published, the Keightley collection of Lawrence letters has been bequeathed to the Royal Academy, and the Victoria and Albert Museum has purchased Keightley's list of the portraits, finished and unfinished, which were left in Lawrence's studio when he died. Certain other papers, in particular those in the archives of Coutts Bank, have escaped previous notice. Inevitably, also, many portraits have changed hands. These facts make a new catalogue desirable. Both Graves and Armstrong included pastels and drawings in their lists, but these are so numerous that they deserve separate treatment, and I have thought it better to deal only with oil paintings here. Such biographical material as the new sources of information contain has been used by Mr. Douglas Goldring in his life of Lawrence, *Regency Portrait Painter*, published in 1951.

I have collected material for a Lawrence catalogue for a period of about four years only, and it cannot claim to be exhaustive. For obvious reasons it has not been possible in that time to see all the portraits I have listed; and I have never been to the United States. I have therefore included only those portraits which I believe from the evidence available to me to be unquestionably by Lawrence or from his studio. In the case of portraits in American collections I have felt unable to admit a large number solely on the evidence of photographs. In one or two cases I have accepted portraits in English collections on the evidence of a strong family tradition without seeing the originals.

I have been so largely helped by friends, by owners and by correspondents that I feel they have done much of the real work for me, and I cannot attempt to express my obligations to them fully. I am in the first place most greatly indebted to Professor Ellis Waterhouse, who has given me advice and information at every stage; and I would like to thank with him Mr. Oliver Millar, who helped me extensively in connection with portraits in the Royal collection and kept me posted with news of portraits he had seen elsewhere, and

ACKNOWLEDGEMENTS

Mr. Frank Simpson, who gave me valuable help in tracing portraits in exhibitions and in the sale room.

I wish to thank the many owners who permitted me to visit their houses, and to reproduce their pictures, and who answered my questions; and I owe especial thanks to the Marquess of Londonderry. In collecting photographs I have received help from so many people that I can only record here my gratitude to them all, and my particular indebtedness to Messrs. Thomas Agnew and Sons, to Monsieur J. Borgaux of the Belgian Embassy in London, to Major Anthony Crofton, to Mr. Clifford Musgrave of the Brighton Art Gallery, and to Mr. H. Schubart of the City Art Gallery, Bristol. For help in taking photographs I thank Mr. W. G. Belsher of the City of Birmingham Museum and Art Gallery. To Mrs. Henry W. Howell, junr., of the Frick Art Reference Library, New York, I am greatly indebted not only for help with photographs but for information of all kinds concerning pictures in collections in the United States.

By gracious permission of Her Majesty the Queen I am allowed to quote passages from the unpublished portion of Farington's Diary. To Sir Owen Morshead, Librarian to Her Majesty the Queen at Windsor Castle, to Mr. Sidney Hutchison, Librarian to the Royal Academy, and to Mr. R. Brooke-Caws, Librarian to Coutts Bank, I am most grateful for access to papers in their care, and for their personal help. I thank also Miss L. N. Simpson, Librarian to Messrs. Knoedler, Mr. Peter Murray of the Witt Library, Mr. Francis Needham, Librarian to the Duke of Wellington, and Mr. David Piper of the National Portrait Gallery; and I thank especially Canon and Mrs. Aston, the Earl of Clanwilliam, Colonel G. R. Codrington, Mr. Lindsay Fleming, and Mrs. Venour, who entrusted Lawrence manuscripts to the post.

I thank the Librarian of the Victoria and Albert Museum and the Trustees of Coutts Bank for their permission to compile appendices from documents in their keeping; and Colonel G. A. Codrington, the Syndics of the Fitzwilliam Museum, Cambridge, and Mr. Reginald Wright of the City of Bath Reference Library for permission to quote from letters.

Last but certainly not least I owe my thanks to my mother for some patient listening and helpful comment; to Dr. Mary Woodall who kindly read the draft of the introduction and Mr. Trenchard Cox who gave me great help in the reading of the proofs; to Professor and Mrs. Owen Hood Phillips and Miss Margaret Stanley-Wrench who took me on expeditions in their motor-cars; and to Mrs. Mary Williams for typing many notes.

ABBREVIATIONS

The following abbreviations have been employed.

Am. Art. Ass.	American Art Association
B.I.	British Institution
C.	Christie's
c.	circa
cat.	catalogue
Commem. Cat.	Commemorative Catalogue
Engr.	Engraved
Gal. Charp.	Galerie Charpentier, Paris
Ex	From the collection of
Exhib.	Exhibited
K.F.R.	Knight, Frank & Rutley
Lith.	Lithograph
Mezz.	Mezzotint
N.Y.	New York
P-B.	Parke-Bernet Galleries
R.A.	Royal Academy of Arts, London
R. & F.	Robinson and Fisher
Repr.	Reproduced
s.	sold
S.	Sotheby's

The word *Replica* has been used to imply that Lawrence painted most of the picture himself and *Repetition* to imply that the picture is probably largely studio work.

NOTE ON THE CATALOGUE

(1) All picture measurements are given in centimetres.

(2) Exhibition records are given up to and including the 2nd Memorial Exhibition of 1833.

(3) Reproduction references are given in full except for *Armstrong*, *Gowan* and *Gower*, for details of which see *Bibliography*, p. 91.

CATALOGUE

ABERCORN, John James, 1st Marquess of (1756–1818).
(1) Possibly R.A. 1793 (80) : 127 × 102 : Marquess of Hamilton, Baron's Court.
(2) Probably before 1810 : 122 × 98 : painted for Sir H. Stewart of Ballygawly House, by whom sold to Lord Claud Hamilton : Sir Richard Proby, Elton Hall.
Repr. Borenius and Hodgson, *Cat. Pictures at Elton Hall*, 1936.
Replica : Marquess of Hamilton, Baron's Court.
(3) After 1805, possibly R.A. 1814 (146) : 236 × 145 : Marquess of Hamilton, Baron's Court.
Repetitions, half-length only : (i) 94 × 76 : formerly Staedel Institute, Frankfort; (ii) 91 × 71 : Smithsonian Institute, Washington.
(1) or (3) *exhib.* B.I. 1833 (12).

ABERDEEN, George, 4th Earl of (1784–1860).
(1) R.A. 1808 (74) : 76 × 63 : Earl of Aberdeen, Haddo House.
Mezz. C. Turner 1809. *Exhib.* B.I. 1830 (41).
Appendix II (2).
(2) R.A. 1830 (116) : 144 × 112 : Ex Sir Robert Peel : Peel Heirlooms s. R. & F. 29/30 November 1917 (89).
Mezz. S. Cousins 1831. *Exhib.* B.I. 1833 (41).
Repr. Lady Frances Balfour, *Life of George 4th Earl of Aberdeen*, 1922.
Variant (largely studio) : 144 × 112 : Viscount Cowdray, Dunecht.

ABERDEEN, Catherine Elizabeth (Hamilton), Countess of (1784–1812).
(1) As Lady Catherine Hamilton c. 1790 : oval 51 × 40 : Duke of Abercorn, London.
(2) R.A. 1803 (64) : size unrecorded : untraced.
(3) c. 1805 : unfinished : Ex Earls of Aberdeen until 1927 : untraced.
Appendix II (3), Appendix III (1).

ABERDEEN, Harriet (Douglas), Countess of (d. 1833).
c. 1815 : 76 × 63 : Ex Earl of Aberdeen 1906 : Sir J. D. Milburn s. C. 10 June 1909 (113) : Sedelmeyer 1911 : Mme Dubernet-Douine s. Gal. Charp. 11/12 April 1946 (22).
Repr. Gowan.

ABERNETHY, John, F.R.S. (1764–1831).
R.A. 1820 (115) : 114 × 112 : St. Bartholomew's Hospital, London (presented by pupils of Abernethy).
Engr. W. Bromley 1827.

ACLAND, Lydia Elizabeth (Hoare), Lady (1786–1856), with her sons, Thomas (1809–98), and Arthur (1811–57).
R.A. 1818 (25) : 154 × 118 : Sir Richard Acland, Bt., Killerton.
Mezz. S. Cousins. *Repr.* Plate 82.

ADAIR, Mrs.
Before 1795 : 76 × 63 : untraced.
Appendix I (3).

ADAM, John (1779–1825).
c. 1827 : 220 × 145 : formerly Government House, Calcutta.
Mezz. C. Turner, 1829.

ADAMS, William Dacres (1775–1862).
c. 1805–10 : 76 × 63 : by family descent to the late Mrs. Katherine Webb, St. Briavels.

AGAR-ELLIS, George Welbore (1797–1833), later 1st Lord Dover. c. 1825 : 127 × 102 : Ex Lord Annaly 1948 : F. Pearson, Foley Manor.
Mezz. W. Brett 1827. *Exhib.* B.I. 1825 (46), 1830 (32*), 1833 (28).

CATALOGUE

AGAR-ELLIS, Lady Georgiana (Howard) (1804–60), later Lady Dover, with her son Henry (1825–66), later 3rd Viscount Clifden.
R.A. 1828 (341) : 127 × 102 : Ex Lord Annaly 1948 : Captain Charles Hepburn.
Mezz. S. Cousins 1831. *Exhib.* B.I. 1830 (32), 1833 (27). *Repr.* Plate 102.

AILESBURY, Henrietta Maria (Noel), Marchioness of (d. 1831). Begun 1809 : 238 × 142 : The National Trust, Attingham Park.
Appendix 3 (2).

AILSA, Margaret, Marchioness of.
See CASSILLIS, Margaret, Lady.

AINSLIE, Master.
R.A. 1794 (199) is described as *Master Ainslie* in a manuscript note in the exhibition catalogue which belonged to J. H. Anderdon and is now in the Library of the Royal Academy of Arts, London.

ALEXANDER I, Emperor of Russia (1777–1825).
1814–1818 : 269 × 174 : H.M. the Queen, Windsor Castle (Waterloo Chamber) : begun London, finished Aix-la-Chapelle.
Exhib. B.I. 1830 (21).

ALLNUTT, John (1773–1863).
R.A. 1799 (5) wrongly described as *Mr. Hunter* : 240 × 142 : Ex 2nd Earl Brassey : Lt.-Comdr. H. Sydney Egerton, Mountfield Court.
Repr. Plate 41.

ALLNUTT, Mrs. John (Elizabeth Garthwaite) (d. 1810), with her daughter.
R.A. 1798 (30) : 242 × 142 : Ex 2nd Earl Brassey : Lt.-Comdr. H. Sydney Egerton, Mountfield Court.
Engr. C. Rolls, 1828, as *The Morning Walk.*

ALLNUTT, Mrs. John (Eleanor Brandram) (d. 1866).
After 1810 : 76 × 63 : Ex Mrs. Knox s. R. & F. 12 December 1907 (175) : Judge Gary s. Am. Art. Ass., N.Y., 28 April 1928 (28) : Scott and Fowles, N.Y., 1931.

ALLNUTT, Miss, daughter of John Allnutt.
Begun 1826 : unfinished : untraced.
Appendix 111 (3).

AMELIA, H.R.H. Princess (1783–1810).
R.A. 1790 (26) : oval 54 × 44 : H.M. the Queen, Windsor Castle.
Appendix 1 (4).
Engr. J. F. Tomkins 1792. *Exhib.* B.I. 1833 (22). *Repr.* Gowan.

AMHERST, William Pitt Amherst, 2nd Baron (1773–1857), Earl Amherst 1826.
(1) R.A. 1805 (150) : untraced.
(2) 1821 : 236 × 145 : painted for the East India Company's Factory at Canton, and presented by the last President of the Factory to Sir George T. Staunton, Bt., 1835 : Earl Amherst (on loan, Ministry of Works, London).
Engr. C. Turner 1824.

ANCRAM, Henrietta (Hobart), Lady (d. 1805).
Unfinished : untraced.
Appendix II (4), Appendix III (4).

ANDERSON, Mr.
c. 1792–3 : untraced.
Appendix I (5).

ANDERSON, Miss Emily (b. *c.* 1805) as Red Riding Hood. R.A. 1822 (300) : 162 × 115 : Ex Anderson family : Henry E. Huntington Art Gallery, San Marino.
Engr. R. J. Lane 1824. *Exhib.* Bristol, Institution for Promotion of Literature, Science and the Fine Arts, 1826. Birmingham, Society of Artists, 1827 (49).
Repr. Collins Baker, *Cat. British Paintings . . . Huntington Library,* 1936.

ANGERSTEIN, John Julius (1735–1823).
(1) With his wife Emily (Crockett).
R.A. 1792 (25) : 256 × 159 : Louvre.
Repr. Plate 13.
(2) *c.* 1792 : head and shoulders, similar to (1), 76 × 63 : Col. Michael Barne, Sotterley Park.
(3) R.A. 1816 (12) : 92 × 71 : William Angerstein s. **c.** 4 July 1896 (110), bt. in : by family descent to J. A. L. Smythies : Lloyd's.
Exhib. B.I. 1830 (37). *Repr.* Plate 75.
Replica : 91 × 71 : painted for George IV, 1828 : presented by William IV to the National Gallery 1836.
Engr. E. Scriven 1829. *Exhib.* B.I. 1833 (33).
Repr. National Gallery, *Illustrations British School,* 1936.
Repetitions : (i) Mrs. Arthur Lehmann, N.Y.; (ii) Morton J. May, St. Louis.
(4) *c.* 1810–15 : 127 × 102 : Ex Victor G. Fischer, by whom presented, 1912, to Metropolitan Museum, N.Y. The identification with Angerstein seems uncertain.

ANGERSTEIN, John (1772/3–1858).
R.A. 1830 (427) : 91 × 71 : by family descent to J. A. L. Smythies.

ANGERSTEIN, Mrs. John (Amelia Lock) 1771–183–) with her son John Julius (1801–1866).
R.A. 1800 (178) as *Mrs. John Angerstein* (the child was added *c.* 1803) : 220 × 164 : Ex William Angerstein s. C. 4 July 1896 (115) : Leopold Hirsch : Lord Michelham 1940.
Exhib. B.I. 1830 (71).

ANGERSTEIN, children of John.

CATALOGUE

R.A. 1808 (195) : 239 × 148 : Mrs. Walter Burns, North Mymms Park.
Exhib. B.I. 1830 (43).

ANGLESEY, Henry William Paget, 1st Marquess of (1768–1854).
R.A. 1817 (24) : 238 × 142 : Marquess of Anglesea, Plas Newydd.
Replica : Apsley House.
Mezz. C. Turner 1828.

D'ANGOULEME, Louis Duc (1775–1844).
1826 : 270 × 176 : H.M. the Queen, Windsor Castle (Waterloo Chamber) : painted in Paris.
Exhib. B.I. 1830 (76).

ANNESLEY, Hon. Arthur (1785–1863), later 10th Viscount Valentia.
1795 : 76 × 63 : Ex Valentia family : Charles Finn Williams, Cincinnati.
Repr. Plate 16.

ANNESLEY, Mrs., and children.
Begun *c.* 1795 : 236 × 145 : Ex Viscount Valentia : Howard Young, N.Y. : Mrs. Walter O. Briggs, Detroit.
Appendix I (6), Appendix 11 (6), Appendix III (5).

ANTROBUS, Edmund (d. 1826), 1st Baronet 1815.
R.A. 1801 (207) : 127 × 102 : Sir Philip Antrobus, Bt., West Amesbury House. *Mezz.* G. Clint.

ANTROBUS, Philip (1755–1816).
c. 1800 : 127 × 102 : Sir Philip Antrobus, Bt., West Amesbury House.
Mezz. G. Clint.

ANTROBUS, Edmund (1792–1870), succeeded to baronetcy 1826, and Gibbs Crawford (1793–1861), sons of John Antrobus, M.P.
c. 1802 : 238 × 142 : Sir Philip Antrobus, Bt., West Amesbury House.
Mezz. G. Clint 1802. *Repr.* Armstrong.

ANTROBUS, Edmund (1792–1870)
c. 1809 : 92 × 71 : Provost's Lodge, Eton College.
Repr. Cust, *Eton Portraits* 1910

APSLEY, Lady Georgiana (Lennox) (d. 1841), later Countess Bathurst.
R.A. 1792 (150) : 76 × 63 : Earl Bathurst, Cirencester House.
Repr. Plate 10.
Appendix I (7).

ARBUTHNOT, Mrs. Charles (Harriet Fane) (1793–1834). R.A. 1817 (150) : 76 × 63 : Private Collection, London.
Mezz. H. W. Giller 1829.

ARGYLL, Caroline (Villiers), Duchess of (d. 1835).
1825 : oval 76 × 63, unfinished : Duke of Richmond and Gordon, Goodwood.

ARMAGH, Archbishop of.
See BERESFORD, John George de la Poer.

ARMISTEAD, Mrs.
c. 1792–3 : untraced.
Appendix I (8).

ARUNDELL of Wardour, John Everard, 9th Baron (1763–1817), and Mary (Burnett-Jones), Lady (d. 1853).
Begun *c.* 1812 : 246 × 157 : Ex Arundell family : s. R. & F. 28 May 1897 (188) : later cut down.
Lady Arundell, 127 × 102, is now in the Toledo Museum of Art (Ex Arthur J. Secor 1923).
Repr. Toledo Museum of Art, *Cat. European Paintings*, 1939.
Appendix III (8).

ASHBURTON, 1st Lord.
See BARING, Alexander.

ASHLEY, Hon. Mrs.
See BAILLIE, Maria Anne.

ATHERLEY, Arthur, M.P. (d. 1844).
R.A. 1792 (209) as *Portrait of an Etonian* : 127 × 102 : Ex Mrs. Killett and Mrs. Pesne, London : Marion Davies, Los Angeles : Los Angeles County Museum.
Repr. Plate 18.
Appendix 1 (9).
Identified by some contemporary critics as *Young Mr. Sheridan.*

AUCHMUTY, Lieut.-Gen. Sir Samuel, K.B. (1756–1822).
1815 : 236 × 147 : presented by subscribers to Government House, Madras.

AUCKLAND, William Eden, 1st Baron (1744–1814).
R.A. 1794 (131) : 127 × 102 : Christ Church, Oxford : painted for the College.
Mezz. W. Dickinson 1796.
Replica : 44 × 34 : Ex A. Levy; Marquess of Lansdowne s. C. 7 March 1930 (49).

BAILLIE, Maria Anne (d. 1891), later Hon. Mrs. Ashley.
Begun 1827 : 127 × 102 : Ex Col. Hugh Baillie :
Mrs. Frank Fussell s. S. 19 June 1935 (142) :
Mrs. Whitelaw (great-niece of sitter), Nairn.
Engr. G. H. Phillips 1842. *Exhib.* B.I. 1833 (3).
Appendix III (9).

BAILLIE, Mathew, M.D. (1761–1823).
Payment before 1806 : 76 × 63 : Royal College of Physicians.
Appendix II (7).

CATALOGUE

BAKER, William of Bayfordbury, M.P. (1743–1824). R.A. 1806 (137) : 127 × 102 : W. L. Clinton Baker, Kineton s. C. 10 July 1953 (84). Appendix II (8).

BAKER, Mrs. William (Sophia Conyers) (d. 1847). Begun *c.* 1812 : 76 × 63 : W. L. Clinton-Baker, Kineton s. C. 10 July 1953 (85). Appendix III (10).

BALFOUR, Blayney Townley (1769–1856). *c.* 1810 : 76 × 63, unfinished : Mrs. Townley-Balfour, Townley Hall. Appendix III (11). *Repr. Country Life,* 30 July 1948.

BANKS, Rt. Hon. Sir Joseph, Bt., P.R.S. (1743–1820). R.A. 1806 (72) : 76 × 63 : The British Museum (Council Room). *Engr.* A. Cardon 1810.

BARIATINSKY, Princess. *See* DUTTON, Hon. Frances Mary.

BARING, Sir Thomas, Bt. (1772–1848), Mary (Sealy) Lady Baring (d. 1846), Mrs. Charles Wall (Harriet Baring) (d. 1838), Francis T. Baring (1796–1866), later Lord Northbrook, and Baring Wall. R.A. 1810 (159) : 156 × 210 : Earl of Northbrook, London. *Exhib.* B.I. 1830 (35). *Repr.* Armstrong.

BARING, Sir Francis, Bt. (1740–1810), John Baring (1730–1816), and Charles Wall. R.A. 1807 (210) : 156 × 226 : Earl of Northbrook, London. *Mezz.* J. Ward. *Exhib.* B.I. 1830 (31). *Repr.* Plate 60.

BARING, Alexander (1774–1848), 1st Lord Ashburton 1835. *c.* 1810 : 127 × 102 : Lord Ashburton, London. *Mezz.* C. E. Wagstaff 1837.

BARING, Mrs. Henry (Maria Matilda Bingham), and her children. R.A. 1821 (106) : 198 × 198 : Ex Comte de Blaisel : Comtesse de Noailles s. C. 16 December 1911 (108) : A. Wertheimer s. C. 18 June 1920 (27) : Mrs. Ogden L. Mills, N.Y. *Repr.* Plate 92. According to family tradition the figure of Henry Baring was painted out at Mrs. Baring's request. A Portrait of Henry Baring 'cut out of a larger picture' was delivered in February 1830 (Appendix III (14)).

BARNARD, Andrew (d. 1807). Before 1806 : 92 × 70 : Earl of Crawford and Balcarres. *Engr.* C. Turner 1809.

Possibly Appendix II (10).

BARRETT, Sarah Moulton (1783–95). R.A. 1795 (75) : 145 × 99 : Ex O. Moulton Barrett: Henry E. Huntington Art Gallery, San Marino, U.S.A. *Repr.* Plate 31.

BARRINGTON, William Wildman, 2nd Viscount (1717–93). R.A. 1792 (109) : 76 × 63 : Viscount Barrington, Nether Lyppiat Manor. *Engr.* C. Knight. *Repr.* Plate 25. Appendix I (10).

BARRINGTON, Hon. Shute (1734–1826), Bishop of Durham. (1) R.A. 1796 (147) : size unrecorded : untraced. (2) R.A. 1816 (47) : 144 × 112 : The Palace, Bishops Auckland. *Mezz.* C. Turner 1817.

BARROW, Rosamund Lady. *See* CROKER, Miss Rosamund.

BARTON, Miss. Begun 1829 : unfinished : untraced. Appendix III (15).

BARWELL, Edward Richard (1786–1846), and Charles Richard (1788–1836). A group of the two brothers, begun before 1806, was unfinished at Lawrence's death. The heads have since been cut out, each 53 × 41, and have passed with the collection of Anthony de Rothschild into the possession of the National Trust, at Ascott, Wing. Appendix II (13), Appendix III (16).

BASSETT, daughters of Lady. Before 1795 : probably 127 × 102 : untraced. Appendix I (II).

BATH, Thomas, 1st Marquess of (1734–1796). R.A. 1796 (163) : 126 × 101 : Marquess of Bath, Longleat. *Engr.* J. Heath.

BATH, Isabella Elizabeth (Byng), Marchioness of (d. 1830), and her children. Begun 1804 : *c.* 236 × 181, unfinished : Marquess of Bath, Longleat. Appendix II (14), Appendix III (17).

BATHURST, Henry, 3rd Earl (1762–1834). (1) *c.* 1818 : 74 × 61 : The Duke of Wellington, Apsley House. (2) *c.* 1820–1823 : 132 × 110 : H.M. The Queen, Windsor Castle (Waterloo Chamber). *Exhib.* B.I. 1830 (6). *Repr.* Armstrong.

BATHURST, Georgiana, Countess. *See* APSLEY, Georgiana, Lady.

BATHURST, Lady Louisa Georgiana (1792–1874).

c. 1810–15 : 61 × 53, unfinished : Earl Bathurst, Cirencester House.

Repr. Earl Bathurst, *Cat. Bathurst Coll.*, 1908.

BATHURST, Hon. Mrs. Seymour (Julia Hankey) (d. 1877).

1828 : 141 × 112 : Earl Bathurst, Cirencester House.

Engr. R. J. Lane 1832. *Repr.* Earl Bathurst. *Cat. Bathurst Coll.*, 1908.

BEAUCLERK, Mrs. Charles.

See OGILVIE, Emily Charlotte.

BEAUMONT, Sir George, Bt., (1753–1827).

(1) R.A. 1793 (15) : untraced.

Appendix I (12).

(2) Sitting April 1808. Farington records, 7 May 1810, that Sir George had sat to Lawrence 'twice or three times for his portrait but it was left in an unfinished state'. Two unfinished portraits of Sir George were included in the Lawrence sale, *c.* 18 June 1831, lot A2, bt. Rhodes, and lot 78, bt. Mitchell.

BEAUMONT, Thomas Wentworth (1792–1841).

c. 1809 : 91 × 71 : Provost's Lodge, Eton College.

Repr. Cust, *Eton Portraits*, 1910.

BECKETT, Rt. Hon. Sir John (1775–1847).

(1) *c.* 1820 : 89 × 70 : Ex Sir Hickman Bacon, Bt. : City Art Gallery, Leeds.

(2) 1820 : 71 × 56, unfinished : Ex Earl of Lonsdale s. Lowther Castle 29 April 1947 (1712); Mrs. J. J. Astor.

Appendix III (19).

BEDFORD, John, 6th Duke of (1766–1839).

R.A. 1822 (113) : 76 × 63 : Duke of Bedford, Woburn Abbey.

Engr. T. A. Dean. *Exhib.* B.I.1830 (60), 1833 (2).

BEDFORD, Georgiana, Duchess of.

See GORDON, Lady Georgiana.

BELFAST, Harriet Anne (Carpenter), Countess of (d. 1860).

R.A. 1830 (71) : 91 × 71 : untraced.

Appendix III (20).

BELGRAVE, Elizabeth Viscountess.

See LEVESON-GOWER, Lady Elizabeth.

BELL, Charles William.

R.A. 1798 (184) : 76 × 63 : Ex Camille Groult, 1913.

Mezz. W. Whiston Barney 1805. *Repr. Les Arts*, June 1905.

BELMORE, Armar Lowry-Corry, 1st Earl of (1740–1802).

Before 1795 : Probably 127 × 102 : untraced.

Appendix I (13).

BENTINCK, Gen. Lord William (1774–1839).

1804 : 127 × 102 : Duke of Portland, Welbeck Abbey.

Engr. Half-length only : H. R. Cook 1813.

Repr. A. Turberville, *A History of Welbeck Abbey and its Owners*, II, 1939.

BENTINCK, Lady Mary (Acheson) (d. 1843).

1807 : 75 × 64 : Duke of Portland, Welbeck Abbey.

Litho : Head and shoulders only : R. J. Lane 1827.

BENTINCK, Lord Charles (1780–1826).

c. 1805 : 76 × 63 : Duke of Portland, Welbeck Abbey.

Repr. A. Turberville, *A History of Welbeck Abbey and its Owners*, II, 1939.

BENTINCK, Lady Charlotte (1775–1862), later Lady Charlotte Greville.

R.A. 1792 (225) : 76 × 63 : Duke of Devonshire, Chatsworth.

Repr. Gowan.

Appendix I (14).

BENTINCK, Lady Mary (1778–1843).

c. 1805 : 75 × 63 : Duke of Portland, Welbeck.

Replica : Head and shoulders only, 59 × 41 : Ex M. M. Zachary s. C. 31 March 1838 (23), bt. Duke of Devonshire : Duke of Devonshire, Chatsworth.

Repr. Gowan.

BERESFORD, Hon. John, M.P. (1738–1805).

R.A. 1791 (97) : untraced.

Appendix I (14).

BERESFORD, William Carr, Viscount (1768–1854).

(1) Begun 1818 : 236 × 146 : painted for the 1st Duke of Wellington : Apsley House.

(2) *c.* 1818 : 236 × 148 : Ex A. J. B. Beresford-Hope : The British Embassy, Lisbon.

Appendix III (20).

BERESFORD, John George de la Poer (1773–1862), Archbishop of Armagh.

R. A. 1830 (100) : 144 × 112 : Marquess of Waterford, Curraghmore.

Mezz. C. Turner 1841.

BERESFORD, Viscountess.

See HOPE, Hon. Mrs. Thomas.

BERKELEY, Captain Sir George Cranfield (1753–1818).

Before 1795 : 72 × 62 : Ex 4th Earl of Berkeley : Burdett-Coutts s. C. 4 May 1922 (45), (repr. cat.) : Knoedler : Dr. James C. Ayer, U.S.A., 1928.

Appendix I (17).

BERKELEY, Lady Emily (Lennox) (d. 1832).
R.A. 1791 (255) : 76 × 63 : by family descent to Agatha, Lady Hindlip, Fernely Heath.
Repr. Plate 8.
Appendix I (16).

BERRI, Marie Caroline, Duchesse de (1798–1870).
1825 : 100 × 74 : Ex Comtesse de Marcellus : Marquis de Forbin : John D. McIlhenny : Mrs. John Wintersteen, Philadelphia.
Repr. Plate 100.
Engr. J. Thomson 1830.

BEWICKE, Mrs. Calverley (Margaret Spearman) (d. 1859).
Before 1795 : 76 × 63 : Ex Bewicke family : Frederick S. Ford, Detroit.
Repr. Plate 9.
Possibly identical with *Mrs. Berwick*, Appendix I (18).

BEXLEY, Nicholas Vansittart, Baron (1766–1851).
(1) R.A. 1823 (124) : 143 × 112 : untraced.
(2) R.A. 1825 (399) : 146 × 112 : Ex Lord Vansittart : Knoedler : D. G. Reid, U.S.A., 1917.
Engr. T. A. Dean 1831.

BINNY, Charles, and his daughters, later Mrs. Parkinson and Mrs. Trevor.
c. 1810–15 : 236 × 181 : Ex Trevor family s. C. 3 May 1902 (60) : Sedelmeyer 1902 : Mme Dubernet-Douine s. Gal. Charp. 11/12 April 1946 (24).
Repr. Gowan.

BIRCH, Lady.
c. 1795 : 76 × 63 : Spink & Son Ltd. 1929.

BISSETT, William (1758–1834), Bishop of Raphoe.
c. 1827 : 127 × 102 : Christ Church, Oxford.
Mezz. C. Turner 1830.

BLACKSHAW, George.
c. 1805 : 76 × 64 : Ex Anon. s. C. 14 March 1924 (24) : Mrs. Jeremiah Milbank, U.S.A. : Honolulu Academy of Arts, Hawaii.
Appendix II (16).

BLANTYRE, Lady.
See LINDSAY, Miss.

BLEAMIRE, William, J.P. (d. 1803).
c. 1800 : 75 × 63 : painted for the Trustees of the Highgate and Hampstead Roads : untraced.
Mezz. J. Young 1803.

BLENCOWE, Mrs. Robert Willis (Penelope Robinson).
Before 1800 : 127 × 102 : Ex Joseph Widener : National Gallery of Art, Washington.
Repr. Paintings at Lynnewood Hall, Philadelphia (privately printed), 1931.

Identified at Washington as *Emma, Lady Robinson*, (*c.* 1802–1874), daughter of Mrs. Blencowe. Stylistically however it must belong to the years before 1800. The identification with Mrs. Blencowe is tentative.

BLESSINGTON, Charles, 1st Earl of.
See MOUNTJOY, Charles, Viscount.

BLESSINGTON, Marguerite (Power), Countess of (1789–1849).
R.A. 1822 (80) : 91 × 70 : Ex Lady Blessington s. Gore House, 15 May 1849 (1032), *bt.* Marquess of Hertford : Wallace Collection.
Engr. J. H. Watt, for *The Amulet*, 1832.
Exhib. B.I. 1833 (10). *Repr.* Plate 96.

BLOOMFIELD, Benjamin, 1st Baron (1768–1846).
(1) After 1820 : 76 × 63 : untraced.
Mezz. C. Turner 1829.
(2) *c.* 1828 : unfinished : untraced.
Appendix III (23).

BLOOMFIELD, John Arthur Douglas (1802–1879), later 2nd Baron Bloomfield.
R.A. 1820 (88) : 74 × 61 : National Portrait Gallery : painted in Vienna 1818.

BLUCHER, Field Marshal Prince von (1742–1819).
1814 : 272 × 181 : H. M. the Queen, Windsor Castle (Waterloo Chamber).
Exhib. B.I. 1830 (7).

BOLLAND, Mr.
Untraced.
Appendix III (24).

BONAR, Mrs. Thomson.
Begun 1813 : 143 × 110 : Ex Thomson-Bonar family s. C. 8 May 1897 (36) : H. J. King s. C. 18 February 1921 (24) : anon s. C. 31 March 1922 (39) : Leggatt : Y. Perdoux, Paris, 1923.
Appendix III (25).

BOUCHERETTE, Ayscoghe, M.P. (d. 1814).
c. 1800 : 76 × 63 : Col. Michael Barne, Sotterley Park.

BOUCHERETTE, Mrs. Ayscoghe (Emily Crockett) (d. 1837).
c. 1795 : 76 × 63 : Ex Newdigate family : Mrs. John S. Newberry, Detroit.

BOUCHERETTE, Ayscoghe, junr. (1792–1857).
c. 1810 : 76 × 63 : Col. Michael Barne, Sotterley Park.
Repr. Plate 67.
Replica : Hon. Mrs. Fitzroy-Newdegate, Arbury.

BOUCHERETTE, Ayscoghe (1792–1857), and Amelia Mary (d. 1874).
Possibly R. A. 1800 (28) : 76 × 63 : Col. Michael Barne, Sotterley Park.

BOULTON, Mr.
Payment 1828 : unfinished.
Appendix III (27).

BOYCE, Mrs.
See MURRAY, Louisa Georgina.

BRADBURNE, John, of Woodlands, Windlesham.
c. 1800 : 75 × 62 : Ex anon. s. C. 19 July 1929 (75) : Agnew : Walker Art Gallery, Liverpool.

BRADBURNE, Mrs. John.
c. 1800 : 76 × 63 : Ex anon. s. C. 5 July 1907 (101) (repr. cat.).

BRADSHAW, Hon. Augustus Cavendish (b. 1768).
Begun *c.* 1805 : unfinished full length : untraced.
Appendix III (28).

BRADSHAW, Hon. Mrs. A. C. (Mary Anne Jeffreys) (d. 1849).
Begun *c.* 1805 : unfinished : untraced.
Appendix 11 (20), Appendix III (29).

BRANDLING, Mrs. C.
Begun 1804 : unfinished : untraced.
Appendix II (21), Appendix III (30).

BRANDLING, Mrs. Charles.
See PEEL, Julia.

BRANDRAM, Mrs. Samuel (Jane Grunwell) (1751–1812).
c. 1810 : 75 × 62 : R.A. Brandram, Bickley.

BRECKNOCK, George Charles Pratt, Earl of (1799–1866), 1st Viscount Bayham, later 2nd Marquess Camden.
c. 1815 : 76 × 63 : Marquess Camden, Bayham Abbey.
Replica : 76 × 63 : Provost's Lodge, Eton College.
Repr. Cust, *Eton Portraits.*

BRISTOL, Frederick William Hervey, 1st Marquess of (1789–1859).
Finished 1827 : 127 × 102 : Marquess of Bristol, Ickworth.
Mezz. J. Bromley for Gage's *Thingoe.*

BROOKE, Miss, later Mrs. Carisbrooke.
Before 1800 : 75 × 62 : Ex S. B. Joel s. C. 31 May 1935 (13) : Barbizon House : Lady Craigmyle.

BROUGHAM and VAUX, Henry Peter, 1st Baron (1778–1868).
c. 1825 : 111 × 79 : Ex Earl of Lincoln s. C. 31 March 1939 (29) : National Portrait Gallery.
Engr. H. Robinson 1832. *Repr.* Plate 114.

BROWNRIGG, Sir Robert, Bt. (1759–1833).
c. 1810 : 76 × 63 : Sir Nicholas Brownrigg, Bt.

Repr. Beatrice, Lady Brownrigg, *Life and Letters of Sir John Moore*, 1923.

BROWNRIGG, Sophia (Bissett), Lady (d. 1837).
After 1820 : 127 × 102 : said to have disappeared from the family possession many years ago.
Engr. W. Ward.

BRYDGES, Sir Harford Jones (1764–1847).
1829 : 76 × 63 : by family descent to Mrs. Lucas-Scudamore, Kentchurch Court.

BUCCLEUCH, Elizabeth (Brudenell-Montagu), Duchess of (1743–1827).
c. 1790 : 76 × 63 : Duke of Buccleuch, Bowhill.
Appendix I (19).

BUCKINGHAMSHIRE, Robert Hobart, 4th Earl of (1760–1816).
(1) *c.* 1795 : 127 × 102 : Ex Earl de Grey and Ripon 1868; P. Jackson Higgs, N.Y., 1930.
Mezz. T. Grozer 1796.
(2) *c.* 1795 : 55 × 50 : Marquess of Bute, Dumfries House.
Head and shoulders similar to (1).

BUCKINGHAMSHIRE, Anne (Pigot), Countess of (d. 1878).
Date and size unrecorded : untraced.
Appendix III (31).

BURDETT, Sir Francis, Bt., M.P. (1770–1844).
Begun *c.* 1793 : 254 × 183 : National Portrait Gallery.
Engr. Half-length only : W. Walker 1805.
Appendix II (25), Appendix III (33).

BURDETT, Sophia Coutts, Lady (1775–1844).
Begun 1793 : 241 × 150 : National Portrait Gallery.
Finished by Evans.

BURGHERSH, Priscilla Anne (Wellesley Pole), Lady (1793–1879), with her son, George Fane (1819–1848), later Lord Burghersh.
1820 : 51 × 45 : Captain F. F. Spicer, Spye Park : painted at Florence.
Engr. G. Longhi, 1823. *Exhib.* B. I. 1833 (13).

BURNEY, Charles, D.D. (1757–1817).
Sitting 1802 : 76 × 63 : The Misses Burney, London, 1952

BURNEY, Charles Parr (1785–1864).
c. 1820–1825 : 75 × 63 : The Misses Burney, London, 1952.

BURRELL, Frances (Wyndham), Lady (d. 1848).
Payment 1829 : 76 × 63 : Lord Leconfield, Petworth.
Appendix III (34).

BURY, Lady Charlotte.
See CAMPBELL, Lady Charlotte.

BUTE, John, 1st Marquess of (1744–1814).
(1) Before 1800 : 76 × 63 : Ex Burdett-Coutts s. C. 4 May 1922 (47) : Marquess of Bute, Dumfries House.
Engr. C. Watson.
(2) *c.* 1805 : 76 × 63, unfinished : Earl of Harrowby, Sandon Hall.
Appendix II (26).

BUTE, Frances (Coutts), Marchioness of (1773–1832).
1806 : 236 × 145 : Earl of Harrowby, Sandon Hall.
Repr. Plate 58.
Appendix II (27).

BYNG, Mrs. George (Harriet Montgomery).
R.A. 1801 (92) : 236 × 145 : Lady Elizabeth Byng, Wrotham Park.

CALLCOTT, Maria (Dundas), Lady (1785–1842).
1819 : 58 × 48, unfinished : National Portrait Gallery : painted in Rome.
Repr. Plate 80.

CALMADY, Emily (d. 1906), and Laura (d. 1894).
R.A. 1824 (99) : 77 × 71 : Ex V. P. Calmady : Collis P. Huntingdon, N.Y. : Metropolitan Museum of Art, N.Y.
Engr. G. T. Doo 1832. *Exhib.* B.I. 1830 (54). *Repr.* Plate 99.

CALVERT, Mrs. Charles (Jane Rowley) (*c.* 1806–67).
Begun *c.* 1825 : unfinished full-length cut down to 61 × 56 : J. C. Calvert, Ockley Court.
Appendix III (35).

CAMBRIDGE, H. R. H. Adolphus Frederick, Duke of (1774–1850).
1818 : 271 × 181 : H.M. the Queen, Windsor Castle (Waterloo Chamber).
Exhib. B.I. 1830 (86).

CAMDEN, John Jeffreys Pratt, 2nd Earl and 1st Marquess (1759–1840).
(1) *c.* 1810–15 : 74 × 61 : National Gallery of Ireland, Dublin.
(2) *c.* 1810–15 : 236 × 145 : Trinity College, Cambridge.
According to Farington Lord Camden sat to Lawrence in August 1811, and again in May 1814.

CAMDEN, George Charles, 2nd Marquess.
See BRECKNOCK, George Charles, Earl of.

CAMPBELL, Lady Charlotte (Campbell) (1775–1861), later Lady Charlotte Bury.
R.A. 1803 (182) : 236 × 145 : Marquess of Hamilton, Barons Court.

CAMPBELL, Lord Frederick (1729–1816).
1815 : 221 × 147 : Society of Dilettanti, London.

Repr. G. A. Macmillan, *Soc. Dilettanti its Regalia and Pictures*, 1932.

CAMPBELL, Thomas, (1777–1844).
c. 1809 : 90 × 70 : National Portrait Gallery.
Engr. Vignette : S. Freeman 1809. *Repr.* Gowan.

CANNING, George, M.P. (1770–1827).
(1) Sitting 1809 : 141 × 110 : Christ Church, Oxford.
Mezz. W. Say 1813.
(2) R.A. 1810 (67) : 89 × 69 : Earl of Haddington.
Repetition : 91 × 71 : The National Trust, Attingham Park.
(3) Possibly R.A. 1825 (83) : 237 × 144 : painted for Canning : 2nd Marquess of Clanricarde : Earl of Harewood, Harewood House.
Repr. Borenius *Cat. Pictures and Drawings at Harewood House*, 1936.
Studio Variants: (i) 249 × 147 : H.M. the Queen, Buckingham Palace, *exhib.* probably B.I. 1830 (90); (ii) 249 × 147 : Walker Art Gallery, Liverpool; (iii) Half-length only : 132 × 105 : H.M. the Queen, Windsor Castle.
(4) Possibly R.A. 1826 (109) : 236 × 147 : Ex Sir Robert Peel : Earl of Harewood : National Portrait Gallery.
Engr. C. Turner 1829. *Exhib.* B.I. 1830 (56).
Tom Moore in his *Diary*, 11 May 1826, quotes a criticism of the R.A. portrait that it 'is like an actor standing before a glass rehearsing a part'. The description best fits this portrait.

CANOVA, Antonio, Marchese di (1757–1821).
R.A. 1816 (184) : 91 × 71 : presented to the sitter by the Prince Regent: bequeathed by Canova's brother to the municipality of Possagno: Gypsoteca Canoviana, Possagno.
Repr. Plate 74.
Replica : 61 × 48 : Earl of Ilchester, London. Many repetitions exist.

CANTERBURY, Charles Manners-Sutton, 1st Viscount (1780–1845).
c. 1810–15 : 127 × 99 : Ex Royal House of Hanover : Landesmuseum, Hanover.

CANTERBURY, Archbishop of.
See HOWLEY, William, MANNERS-SUTTON, Charles, MOORE, Dr. John.

CAPEL, Mary-Anne, later Lady Carrington.
Begun 1827 : 91 × 71 : Ex A. Wertheimer s. C. 18 June 1920 (28).
Engr. C. Rolls, for *Friendships Offering*, 1832. *Exhib.* B.I. 1830 (72).

CAPO D'ISTRIA, Joannes, Count (1776–1831).
1819 : 130 × 104 : H.M. the Queen, Windsor

Castle (Waterloo Chamber) : painted at Vienna.
Exhib. B.I. 1830 (14).

CAPPER, Mr.
Before 1795 : untraced.
Appendix I (20).

CARBERY, John, 6th Baron (1765–1845).
Before 1806 : unfinished full-length : untraced.
Appendix II (30), Appendix III (36).

CARLISLE, George, 6th Earl of (1773–1848).
After 1825 : 269 × 176 : George Howard, Castle Howard.
Head begun by Lawrence : finished by Tomlinson.
Appendix III (37).

CAROLINE, Princess of Wales (1768–1821).
(1) 1798 : 127 × 102 : Victoria and Albert Museum.
Repr. Armstrong.
(2) With the Princess Charlotte.
R.A. 1802 (72) : 305 × 206 : H.M. the Queen, Buckingham Palace.
Repr. Gower.
(3) 1804 : 140 × 112 : National Portrait Gallery.
Repr. Plate 52.

CARRINGTON, Sir Codrington Edmund (1769–1849).
c. 1801 : 74 × 62 : Victoria and Albert Museum.
Exhib. B.I. 1830 (47).

CARRINGTON, Paulina (Belli), Lady.
c. 1801 : 74 × 62 : Victoria and Albert Museum.

CARRINGTON, Mary-Anne, Lady.
See CAPEL, Mary-Anne.

CARTER, Miss Mary (d. 1797), later Lady William Beauclerk.
1789 : 76 × 63 : Col. O. Sutton Nelthorpe, Scawby.

CASSILIS, Margaret (Erskine), Lady (d. 1848), later Marchioness of Ailsa.
Begun before 1806 : unfinished whole length : untraced.
Appendix II (31), Appendix III (38).

CASTLEREAGH, Henry Robert, Viscount.
See LONDONDERRY, Robert, 2nd Marquess of.

CAULFIELD, Lady Emily (1808–29).
Date and size unrecorded : untraced.
Appendix III (39).

CAVENDISH, Children of Lord George, later 1st Earl of Burlington, William (1783–1812), George Henry (1784–1809), Anne (1787–1871), later Lady Charles Fitzroy.

R.A. 1790 (202) : 245 × 210 : Lord Chesham.
Repr. Plate 15.
Appendix I (21).

CAVENDISH, Lady George.
See LASCELLES, Lady Louisa.

CAWDOR, John Frederick Campbell, 2nd Baron and 1st Earl (1790–1860).
Payment 1829 : 76 × 63, unfinished : untraced.
Appendix III (41).

CAWDOR, Elizabeth (Thynne), Countess of (d. 1866).
1827 : 64 × 61, unfinished : Earl of Cawdor, Stackpoole Court.
Engr. Vignette : C. Marr, for *The Amulet*, 1832.
Appendix III (40).

CECIL, Lord Brownlow (1795–1867), later 2nd Marquess of Exeter, Lord Thomas (b. 1797), and Lady Sophia (d. 1823), later Lady Sophia Pierrepont.
Begun *c.* 1800 : 156 × 123, unfinished : Marquess of Exeter, Burghley House.
Appendix III (63).

CHAPLIN, Francis, M.P.
Finished 1825 : 91 × 71 : C. R. Sutton, Newbury.
Exhib. B.I. 1830 (80).
Appendix III (42).

CHARLEMONT, Francis William Caufield, 2nd Earl of (1775–1863), Anne Bermingham, Countess of (d. 1876), and child.
R.A. 1812 (108) : cut down 1894.
(1) *Lord Charlemont* : 76 × 63 : National Gallery, Dublin.
(2) *Lady Charlemont and Child* : said to be in America.

CHARLES X, King of France (1757–1836).
1825 : 268 × 175 : H.M. the Queen, Windsor Castle (Waterloo Chamber) : painted in Paris.
Engr. C. Turner 1828. *Exhib.* B.I. 1830 (19).

CHARLES, Archduke, of Austria (1771–1847).
1818 : 270 × 176 : H.M. the Queen, Windsor Castle (Waterloo Chamber): painted at Vienna.
Exhib. B.I. 1830 (20). *Repr.* Plate 88.
Replica : Delivered to Prince Esterhazy for despatch to the Archduke Charles, 1831.

CHARLES, Archduchess, of Austria (Henrietta of Nassau-Weilburg).
1819 : 270 × 176 : formerly Imperial Collection, Vienna : painted at Vienna.
Repr. W. John, *Erzherzog Karl, der Feldherr und sein Armee*, 1913.

CHARLES, daughter of the Archduke.
See MARIA THERESIA, Princess.

CHARLOTTE, Queen (1744–1818).
R.A. 1790 (100) : 239 × 147 : Ex Lawrence
s. C. 18 June 1831 (133) : Lord Ridley s. C.
8 July 1927 (59) : National Gallery.
Repr. Plate 2. *Exhib.* B.I. 1833 (40).
Appendix I (67).

CHARLOTTE, Princess (1796–1817).
(1) With the Princess of Wales.
R.A. 1802 (72) : 305 × 206 : H.M. the Queen,
Buckingham Palace.
(2) *c.* 1802 : 76 × 63 : H.M. the Queen,
Windsor Castle.
Engr. M. A. Bourlier 1806. *Repr.* Gower.
(3) Sitting 1817 : R.A. 1821 (70) : 102 × 81 :
H.M. the King of the Belgians.
Engr. R. Golding, 1822. *Repr.* Plate 91.
Repetitions : (i) H.M. The Queen, Windsor
Castle ; (ii) Formerly the Earl of Ilchester,
Abbotsbury : destroyed by fire 1912.

CHOLMONDELY, Mr.
Before 1795 : untraced.
Appendix I (22).

CLAM-MARTINICS, Selina, Countess
See MEADE, Lady Selina.

CLANWILLIAM, Richard Meade, 3rd Earl of
(1795–1879).
R.A. 1824 (98) : 220 × 145 : Earl of Clanwilliam, London.

CLARENCE, William, Duke of (1765–1837), later
King William IV.
(1) Possibly R.A. 1793 (63) : 127 × 102 : Lord
De L'Isle and Dudley, Penshurst.
Replica : 127 × 102 : Ex Burdett-Coutts s. C.
4 May, 1922 (42) (*repr.* cat.) : Viscount Bear-
stead : The National Trust, Upton House.
(2) 1827 : 254 × 167 : H.M. the Queen, Buckingham Palace.
Mezz. J. E. Coombs 1836. *Exhib.* B.I. 1833
(36).

CLARKE, Richard (1739–1830).
R.A. 1827 (422) : 142 × 112 : Guildhall,
London.
Commissioned by the Corporation of London,
1825.
Mezz. J. S. Davis 1829.

CLEMENTS, Harriet.
c. 1805 : 126 × 101 : Ex T. L. Fitz Hugh :
Leopold Hirsch s. C. 11 May 1934 (100) : Lord
Brocket : Frost & Reed, Bristol, 1937.
Appendix II (35).

CLEVELAND, Elizabeth, Duchess of.
See DARLINGTON, Elizabeth, Countess of.

CLIVE, Hon. Edward (1785–1848), later 2nd Earl
of Powis.

c. 1803 : 76 × 63 : Provost's Lodge, Eton
College.
Repr. Cust, *Eton Portraits,* 1910.

CLIVE, Hon. Robert (1789–1854).
Begun 1808 : 74 × 62, unfinished : Earl of
Plymouth, Oakley Park.
Appendix III (45).

CLIVE, Lady Harriet (1797–1869), later Baroness
Windsor.
Begun *c.* 1823 : 142 × 112 : the Earl of Ply-
mouth, Oakley Park.
Mezz. S. Cousins 1840.
Appendix III (44).

CLIVE, Lady Lucy.
1826 : unfinished : untraced.
Appendix III (43).

CLUDDE, Mrs. William (Anna Maria Jeffreys)
(1762–1835).
1806–1810 : 76 × 63 : Col. E. R. H. Herbert,
Orleton.
Probably identical with *Mrs. Chudd.*
Appendix II (34), Appendix III (46).

CODRINGTON, Vice-Admiral Sir Edward, G.C.B.
(1770–1851).
Finished 1826 : 76 × 63 : Col. G. R. Codring-
ton, Winterslow.
Mezz. C. Turner, 1830. *Exhib.* B. I. 1830 (81).
Appendix III (47).

CODRINGTON, Henry John (1808–1877), later
Admiral Sir Henry.
1829 : 75 × 62, unfinished : Capt. W. M.
Codrington.
Appendix III (48).

COKE, Thomas W., M.P. (1752–1842), later 1st
Earl of Leicester.
(1) Sitting 1807 : 243 × 112 : Shire Hall, Norwich.
Mezz. C. Turner, 1814.
(2) *c.* 1818 : 92 × 71 : Ex Mrs. A. M. Roscoe :
Walker Art Gallery, Liverpool.
Mezz. C. Turner 1818.

COLE, General Sir Galbraith Lowry (1772–1842).
c. 1811 : 76 × 62 : Ex Lady Lucas s. C.
26 May 1922 (76) : Knoedler : Edwin Mallin-
krodt, St. Louis, 1923.
Engr. C. Picart 1816.

COMBERMERE, Sir Stapleton Cotton, 1st Viscount
(1773–1865).
Begun 1815 : 238 × 146 : Ex anon. s. C.
30 July 1924 (230) : finished by Lane.
Appendix III (49).

CONSALVI, Ercole, Cardinal (1757–1824).
1819 : 269 × 178 : H.M. the Queen, Windsor
Castle (Waterloo Chamber) : painted at Rome.
Exhib. B.I. 1830 (8). *Repr.* Plate 89.

CONYNGHAM, Elizabeth (Denison), Marchioness (1766/7–1861).
(1) R.A. 1802 (176) : 235 × 149 : trustees of the Londesborough settled Estates (on loan City of Birmingham Museum and Art Gallery). *Repr.* Plate 50.
(2) Sitting 1823 : 127 × 102 : Marquess Conyngham.

CONYNGHAM, Lord Francis (1797–1876), later 2nd Marquess Conyngham.
R.A. 1823 (84) : 76 × 63 : Marquess Conyngham.

CONYNGHAM, Lady Elizabeth (1799–1839), later Marchioness of Huntly.
1821–4 : 91 × 71 : Ex Marquess Conyngham : C. E. Gulbenkian (on loan National Gallery of Art, Washington).

CONYNGHAM, Lady Maria (d. 1843), later Lady Somerville.
c. 1825 : 91 × 71 : Ex Marquess Conyngham; Mrs. James P. Donahue, N.Y.

COOPER, Hon. Cropley Ashley (1768–1851), later 6th Earl of Shaftesbury.
R.A. 1811 (13) : 124 × 99 : Earl of Shaftesbury, St. Giles House.
Mezz. C. Turner 1812.

COOPER, Sir Astley Paston, Bt. (1768–1841).
R.A. 1828 (263) : 142 × 112 : Royal College of Surgeons.
Mezz. S. Cousins, 1830. *Repr. The Connoisseur,* June 1928.

COOPER, Robert Bransby, M.P. (1762–1845).
Sitting 1813 : 76 × 63 : untraced.
Engr. W. T. Fry 1820.

COPLEY, Juliana (d. 1834), later Lady Watson.
1789 : 75 × 62 : Ex Sir W. J. Watson s. C. 25 June 1904 (108) : Sir Berkeley Sheffield s. C. 16 July 1943 (75) (*repr.* cat.) : Mrs. J. V. Rank, Godstone.

CORNWALLIS, Louisa, Marchioness of.
See GORDON, Lady Louisa.

COTTON, Joseph, F.R.S. (1745–1825).
c. 1810 : 125 × 99 : Ex A. E. Cotton s. C. 11 March 1932 (117) : Hon. Mrs. Chaplin, London.
Mezz. C. Turner 1818.

COTTON, Mrs. Joseph (Sarah Harrison).
c. 1810 : 125 × 99 : Ex A. E. Cotton s. C. 11 March 1932 (118).
Mezz. C. Turner 1825.

COWPER, Peter Leopold, 5th Earl (1778–1837).
R.A. 1802 (56) : 127 × 99 : Cowper Collection, Panshanger.

COWPER, Emily, Countess.
See LAMB, Lady Emily.

COWPER, Lady Emily (1810–72), later Lady Ashley and Countess of Shaftesbury.
R.A. 1814 (271) : within an oval, probably 76 × 63 : Ex Lady Edith Ashley (1900).
Engr. T. Wright 1830 as *the Rosebud. Exhib.* B.I. 1830 (22). *Repr.* Gower.

CRADOCK, Lieut.-Gen. Sir John (1762–1839), later 1st Baron Howden.
c. 1803 : 127 × 102 : Mrs. B. F. Jones, Pittsburgh, s. P-B., N.Y., 4/5 December 1941 (81).
Mezz. W. Say, 1805.

CRAVEN, William Craven, 1st Earl of (1770–1825).
Payment 1802 : 236 × 145 : Cornelia, Countess of Craven, Hamsted Marshall.
Appendix II (37), Appendix III (50).

CREMORNE, Thomas Dawson, Viscount (1725–1813).
c. 1790 : 249 × 145 : Ex Earl of Dartrey : Lt.-Comdr. C. Windham, Cerne Abbas (on loan City of Bristol Art Gallery).
Engr. C. Knight 1794. *Repr.* Plate 6.
Appendix I (23).

CREMORNE, Philadelphia Hannah (Freame), Viscountess (*c.* 1740–1826).
R.A. 1789 (100) : 249 × 145 : Ex Earl of Dartrey : Lt.-Comdr. C. Windham, Cerne Abbas (on loan City of Bristol Art Gallery).
Repr. Plate 1.
Appendix I (24).

CREWE, John Crewe, 1st Lord (1742–1829).
c. 1810 : 76 × 63 : Marchioness of Crewe, London.
Mezz. W. Say.

CREWE, Frances Anne (Greville), Lady (d. 1818).
c. 1810 : 76 × 63 : Marchioness of Crewe, London.
Mezz. W. Say, 1816.

CROKER, Rt. Hon. John Wilson, M.P. (1780–1857).
R.A. 1825 (140) : 75 × 66 : National Gallery of Ireland, Dublin.
Mezz. S. Cousins 1829. *Exhib.* B.I. 1830 (57). *Repr.* Armstrong.

CROKER, Rosamund Hester Elizabeth (b. Pennell), (1810–1906), later Lady Barrow.
R.A. 1827 (26) : 76 × 63 : Ex Rt. Hon. J. W. Croker : J. Pierpont Morgan : Albright Art Gallery, Buffalo.
Mezz. S. Cousins 1832. *Exhib.* B.I. 1830 (58).

CROUCH, Mrs. (Anna Maria Phillips) (1763–1805).
c. 1790 : 76 × 63 : Ex Camille Groult s. Gal. Charp. 27 April 1951 (25), as *Hoppner.*
A variant *engr.* W. Ridley 1792.

CATALOGUE

CUMBERLAND, Prince George of (1819–1878).
1828 : 254 × 140 : H.M. the Queen, Buckingham Palace.
Exhib. B.I. 1830 (74), 1833 (5). *Repr*. Plate 117.

CURRAN, John Philpot (1750–1817).
(1) R.A. 1800 (54) : 76 × 62 : National Gallery of Ireland, Dublin.
Repr. Armstrong.
(2) 1800 : 76 × 63 : Earl Grey, Howick.
Mezz. J. R. Smith, 1801. *Repr*. Plate 56.

CURTIS, Sir William, 1st Bt. (1752–1829).
(1) R.A. 1812 (103) : 243 × 112 : Sir Peter Curtis, Bt., Kimbridge House.
Engr. W. Sharp 1814. *Repr*. Plate 112.
(2) R.A. 1824 (291) : 90 × 70 : H.M. the Queen, Windsor Castle.
Mezz. W. Say 1831.

CURTIS, James (1750–1835).
R.A. 1804 (121) : 91 × 71 : untraced.
Mezz. Anon. (private plate).

CUTHBERT, Mr.
Before 1820 : 236 × 145 : Ex Sedelmeyer 1897 : C. Groult 1913.
Repr. Sedelmeyer Gallery, *Illustrated Catalogue*, 4th Series, 1897.

CUTHBERT, Mrs.
R.A. 1817 (155) : 142 × 112 : Ex Sedelmeyer 1897: Carlos de Beistegui : Louvre. *Repr*. Gowan.

DAINTREY, Midshipman Michael.
1813 : 76 × 63 : by family descent to Lt.-Col. Ian Anderson.

DALRYMPLE, Elizabeth, later Lady Prendergast.
c. 1801 : 76 × 63, unfinished : Ex Dalrymple family : Agnew : Count Contini, Rome : Knoedler, London.
Appendix II (38), Appendix III (124).

DANCE, George, R.A. (1741–1825).
c. 1800 : 75 × 62 : Ex anon. s. C. 25 April 1913 (98).
Repr. *The Connoisseur*, October 1914.

DANSEY, Mr.
R.A. 1788 (147) : probably 76 × 63 : untraced.
Engr. J. Heath.
Appendix I (26).

DARLINGTON, Elizabeth (Russell), Countess of (1777–1861), later Duchess of Cleveland.
c. 1813 : 228 × 150 : said to have hung at Raby Castle until 1913 : Albert Belleroche : Agnew : Nate B. Spingold, N.Y.

DARNLEY, Emma Jane (Parnell), Countess of (1804–84).
c. 1825 : 62 × 51, unfinished : said to have been purchased at one of the Lawrence sales (no sketch entitled *Countess of Darnley* appears in the catalogues) : Robert Vernon : Tate Gallery.

DARTMOUTH, William, 4th Earl of.
See LEGGE, Hon. William.

DASHWOOD, Anna Maria (d. 1857), later Marchioness of Ely.
c. 1805 : 76 × 63 : Ex Marquess of Ely s. C. 25 July 1891 (68) : Agnew : R. Hall-McCormick, s. N.Y., 15 April 1920 (62). Appendix II (40).

DAVENPORT, Mrs. Davies (Charlotte Sneyd).
1827 : size unrecorded : untraced.
Appendix III (51).

DAVY, Sir Humphrey, Bt., P.R.S. (1778–1829).
R.A. 1821 (171) : 132 × 92 : The Royal Society.
Engr. R. Newton 1830.

DAY, Harriet Maria, later Mrs. Ichabod Wright.
R.A. 1791 (122) : 76 × 63 : Ex A. S. Wright s. C. 1 July 1899 (103) as *Reynolds* : Cronier sale Paris, 1903 : R. B. Angus, Montreal : Montreal Museum of Fine Arts.
Appendix I (25).

DELAVAL, Sarah Hussey (1795–1825), later Mrs. James Gunman.
c. 1820 : 76 × 63 : R. G. E. Jarvis, London.

DERBY, Edward, 13th Earl of.
See STANLEY, Lord Edward Smith.

DERBY, Eliza, Countess of.
See FARREN, Eliza.

DE GREY, Thomas, 1st Earl.
See GRANTHAM, Thomas, 3rd Lord.

DE GREY, Henrietta Frances, Countess.
See GRANTHAM, Henrietta Frances, Lady.

DE TABLEY, Georgina Mary, Lady.
See LEICESTER, Georgiana Mary, Lady.

DE VISME, Emily (d. 1873) later Lady Murray.
c. 1794 : 127 × 102 : Ex Miss G. L. Murray s. C. 25 June 1904 (19) : S. B. Joel s. C. 31 May 1935 (12) : H. J. Joel, St. Albans.
Engr. W. Bond 1794, as *The Woodland Maid*.

DEVONSHIRE, William Spencer Cavendish, 6th Duke of (1790–1858).
(1) Sitting 1811 : 145 × 119 : Ex Admiral Sir A. W. Clifford : Lord Dormer, Grove Park.
Repr. Plate 66.
(2) Probably R.A. 1824 (146) : 76 × 63 : H.M. The Queen, Windsor Castle.
Replica : 76 × 63 : George Howard, Castle Howard.

DEVONSHIRE, Elizabeth, Duchess of.
See FOSTER, Lady Elizabeth.

D'EWES, Miss Anne.
See STRATTON, Mrs. G. F.

34

CATALOGUE

DINGWALL, Mrs.
  c. 1825 : unfinished : untraced.
  Appendix III (52).
DONEGAL, Harriet Anne, Marchioness of.
  See BELFAST, Harriet Anne, Countess of.
DOTTIN, Abel Rous M.P. (d. 1852), Mrs. Dottin
  (Miss Burnett-Jones), and Mrs. Cumberbatch
  (Dorothy Burnett-Jones).
  Begun 1798 : unfinished portrait group : un-
  traced.
  Appendix II (43), Appendix III (53).
DOUGLAS, Archibald (1748–1827), Baron Douglas
  of Douglas 1790. *c.* 1790 : 76 × 63 : Duke of
  Buccleuch, Bowhill. Appendix I (27) or (28).
DOUGLAS, Rt. Hon. Sylvester (1743–1823), later
  Lord Glenbervie.
  R.A. 1792 (183) : 127 × 102 : untraced.
  Engr. E. Harding, 1794.
DOUGLAS, Harriet (b. 1790).
  Sitting 1828–9 : unfinished : untraced.
  Appendix III (54).
DOVER, George Welbore, Lord.
  See AGAR-ELLIS, George Welbore.
DOVER, Georgiana, Lady.
  See AGAR-ELLIS, Lady Georgiana.
DOWNE, John Christopher Dawnay, 5th Viscount
  (1764–1832).
  Begun *c.* 1810 : 236 × 145 : Viscount Downe,
  Wykeham Abbey.
  Mezz. T. Lupton.
DOYLE, Major.
  Before 1795 : untraced.   Appendix I (29).
DROOP, Mrs. J. A. (Miss Richmond).
  Begun 1823 : 76 × 63 : Ex Henry Richmond,
  Stamford Hill : finished by Lane.
  Litho. R. J. Lane.   Appendix III (55).
DRUMMOND, Lady Clementina Sarah (1786 1865),
  later Lady Willoughby D'Eresby.
  c. 1805 : 231 × 143, unfinished : Earl of
  Ancaster, Grimsthorpe Castle.
  Repr. Arundel Club Reproductions, 1915.
  Appendix II (45), Appendix III (155).
DRUMMOND, Lady Elizabeth.
  See MANNERS, Lady Elizabeth.
DUCIE, Thomas, 1st Earl of.
  See MORETON, Hon. Thomas.
DUGDALE, Mrs. Stratford.
  See SYKES, Elizabeth, Lady.
DUNCANNON, Maria, Lady.
  See FANE, Lady Maria.
DUNDAS, Margaret (Bruce), Lady (1715–1802).
  1799 : 127 × 102 : Marquess of Zetland,
  Aske.
  Mezz. G. Clint. *Repr.* Plate 40.

DUNDAS, Thomas Dundas, 1st Baron (1741–
  1820).
  1817 : 76 × 63 : Society of Dilettanti London.
  Mezz. C. Turner, 1822. *Repr.* G. A. Macmillan,
  Soc. Dilettanti its Regalia and Pictures, 1932.
  Replica : 76 × 63 : Earl Fitzwilliam, Milton
  Park.
DUPRE, James (1778–1870).
  Begun before 1806, but apparently completed
  some years later : 127 × 112 : Lt.-Col. A. M.
  Grenfell, London.
  Appendix II (46).
DUPRE, Mrs. James (Madelina Maxwell) (1779–
  1821).
  Sitting 1802 : 236 × 147 : Lt.-Col. A. M.
  Grenfell, London.
  Appendix II (47).
DURHAM, John George, 1st Earl of.
  See LAMBTON, John George.
DURHAM, Louisa, Countess of.
  See LAMBTON, Lady Louisa.
DURHAM, Bishop of.
  See BARRINGTON, Shute, MILDERT, William
  Van.
DUTTON, Hon. Frances Mary (d. 1807), later
  Princess Bariatinsky.
  c. 1806 : unfinished : untraced.
  Appendix III (12).
DYSART, Countess of.
  See MANNERS, Lady Louisa.
EDEN, James (1796–1800).
  1800 : oval 63 × 54 : Sir Timothy Eden, Bt.,
  Fritham House : painted after death.
EDWARDS, Samuel (*c.* 1747–1815).
  Before 1805 : 91 × 71 : by family descent to
  Mrs. A. W. Vivian-Neal, Poundisford Park.
EGERTON, Lord Francis.
  See LEVESON-GOWER, Lord Francis.
EGERTON, Mrs. Wilbraham (Elizabeth Sykes)
  (d. 1853).
  Begun *c.* 1805 : unfinished : untraced.
  Appendix III (58).
ELDON, John Scott, 1st Earl of (1751–1838).
  (1) 1798 : 77 × 65 : Earl of Eldon, Rackenford
  Manor.
  Mezz. J. Smith 1800.
  (2) R.A. 1825 (118) : 140 × 109 : Ex Sir
  Robert Peel : Peel Heirlooms s. R. & F.
  29/30 November 1917 (97) : Viscount Cowdray.
  (3) R.A. 1828 (463) : 92 × 70 : H.M. The
  Queen, Windsor Castle.
  Mezz. T. Doo, 1828. *Repr.* Gower.
  Studio Repetition : 91 × 71 : National Portrait
  Gallery.

35

CATALOGUE

ELLENBOROUGH, Edward Law, 1st Baron (1750–1818).
R.A. 1806 (35) : 146 × 112 : Ex Lord Ellenborough s. S. 11 June 1947 (82) : Mr. Justice Pearce, London.
Mezz. C. Turner 1809.
Appendix II (48).

ELLENBOROUGH, Anne (Towry), Lady (d. 1843).
R.A. 1813 (158) : 73 × 62 : Ex Lord Ellenborough s. C. 28 May 1895 (144) : George A. Hearn : Metropolitan Museum, New York.
Repr. Metropolitan Museum, *The George A. Hearn Gift*, 1906.

ELLENBOROUGH, Jane Elizabeth (Digby), Lady (1807–1881).
c. 1825 : 61 × 51 : Ex J. W. Wilson : Camille Groult s. Gal. Charp. 27 April 1951 (27).

ELLIOT, Sir Gilbert (1751–1814), later 1st Earl of Minto.
R.A. 1794 (78) : 73 × 62 : Ex Burdett-Coutts s. C. 4 May 1922 (43) : Lady Violet Astor, London.

ELLIOT, Rt. Hon. William (d. 1818).
Probably after 1810 : 76 × 63 : Earl of Minto, Melgund.

ELPHINSTONE, Hon. Mountstuart (1779–1859).
1829 : 243 × 112 : Elphinstone College, Bombay : finished by Simpson.
Mezz. C. Turner 1833.
Replica : 120 × 73 : Lord Elphinstone, Carbery Tower.
Appendix III (59).

ELY, Anna Maria, Marchioness of.
See DASHWOOD, Anna Maria.

ENGLEFIELD, Sir Henry C., Bt. (1752–1822)
R.A. 1813 (28) : 91 × 71 : Society of Dilettanti, London.
Engr. W. Bromley, 1816. *Repr.* G. A. Macmillan, *Soc. Dilettanti its Regalia and Pictures*, 1932.

ERRINGTON, Julia, Lady.
See MACDONALD, Julia.

ERSKINE, Hon. Thomas (1750–1823), later 1st Baron Erskine.
R.A. 1802 (184) : 76 × 63 : Ex Charles Moore : Miss Carrick Moore : Lincoln's Inn.
Mezz. G. Clint 1803. *Repr.* Plate 55.
Replica : 76 × 63 : Ex Sir Robert Peel : Peel Heirlooms s. R. & F. 29/30 November 1917 (85).

ESDAILE, Mr.
1829 : unfinished : untraced.
Appendix III (60).

ESSEX, George Capell, 5th Earl of (1757–1839).
Finished 1829 : 75 × 62 : possibly Earl of Essex s. Cassiobury, June 1922 (740).
Appendix III (61).

ESTEN, Harriet Pye (Bennett) (1768?–1868), later Mrs. Scott-Waring.
Payment 1800 : untraced.
Appendix II (51), Appendix III (148).

EXETER, Henry Cecil, 10th Earl of (1754–1804), Sarah (Hoggins), Countess of (1773–1797), and Lady Sophia Cecil (d. 1823), later Lady Sophia Pierrepont.
R.A. 1797 (74) : 218 × 146 : Marquess of Exeter, Burghley House.

EXETER, Elizabeth (Burrell), Marchioness of, (d. 1837).
R.A. 1802 (17) : 239 × 146 : Marquess of Exeter, Burghley House.
Mezz. S. W. Reynolds 1803.

EXETER, Isabella (Poyntz), Marchioness of (1803–1879).
1829 : 127 × 102 : Marquess of Exeter, Burghley House : finished by Shee.
Engr. C. W. Wass.
Appendix III (62).

EXMOUTH, Edward, 1st Viscount.
See PELLEW, Admiral Sir Edward.

FAIRLIE, Mrs. John (Louisa Purves) (d. 1843).
Sitting 1827 : unfinished : untraced.
Appendix III (64).

FALMOUTH, Marie Anne (Bankes), Countess of (1789–1864).
c. 1810 : 76 × 63 : H. J. R. Bankes, Kingston Lacy.

FANE, Lady Maria (d. 1834), later Lady Duncannon.
c. 1804 : 236 × 145 : Earl of Bessborough, Stanton.
Repr. J. Gore, *Creevey's Life and Times*, 1934.
Appendix II (54), Appendix III (57).

FANE, Lady Georgiana (d. 1874).
1806 : 142 × 95 : bequeathed by sitter to the National Gallery : Tate Gallery.
Mezz. C. Turner 1826. *Exhib.* B.I. 1830 (38).
Repr. Armstrong.
Appendix II (53).

FANE, Master George (1819–1848).
c. 1821 : circular, diameter 34 : Ex James Price s. C. 15 June 1895 (53), bt. Agnew.

FARINGTON, Joseph, R.A. (1747–1821).
(1) R.A. 1796 (164) : 75 × 62 : Ex Miss Susan ffarington s. S. 17 March 1948 (59).
Repr. Plate 23.
(2) R.A. 1808 (134) : 91 × 71 : Ex Anon s.

CATALOGUE

R. & F. 1 June 1911 (118): C. Brunner, Paris : Museu Nacional de Bellas Artes, Buenos Aires. *Engr.* H. Meyer 1814. *Repr. The Farington Diary*, ed. Grieg, 1923, Vol. I.

FARNHAM, John Maxwell, 5th Baron (1767–1829). Begun 1826 : 146 × 112 : Lord Farnham, Cavan. Appendix III (65).

FARREN, Eliza (1759–1829), later Countess of Derby. R.A. 1790 (171) : 238 × 147 : Ex Earl of Wilton : Ludwig Neumann : J. Pierpont Morgan : Edward S. Harkness : Metropolitan Museum, N.Y.
Engr. F. Bartolozzi, 1792. *Repr.* Plate 3.
Appendix I (31).

FAWCETT, John (1768–1837). Begun 1828 : 73 × 61 : Ex Robert Vernon by whom commissioned : National Gallery (on loan National Portrait Gallery). Appendix III (66).

FINCH, Mrs. According to Armstrong, R.A. 1793 (235), *Portrait of a Lady* was described by a contemporary critic as 'The Celebrated Mrs. Finch'.

FITZGERALD, Mary Frances Purcell- (Fitzgerald) (d. 1855). 1825 : 76 × 63, unfinished : by family descent to Mrs. Mary d'Ardia Carraciolo, Waterford. Appendix III (67).

FITZWILLIAM, William Wentworth-Fitzwilliam, 4th Earl (1748–1833). *c.* 1827 : 220 × 145 : Earl Fitzwilliam, Wentworth Woodhouse. *Repr.* A. S. Turberville, *A History of Welbeck Abbey and its Owners*, II, 1939. Appendix III (68).

FLUDYER, Children of Sir Samuel, 2nd Bt. (1759–1833). 1806 : 239 × 148 : Ex Mrs. Ogilvie-Grant 1918 : Agnew : Marshall Field, N.Y.; San Paolo, Art Gallery. Appendix II (57).

FORBES, Sir William (1739–1806). 1803 : probably 76 × 63 : untraced. Farington states, 20 August 1803, 'Lawrence has painted one of his best heads—a portrait of Sir Wm. Forbes. He finished it on Wednesday last.'

FOSTER, Lady Elizabeth (Hervey) (1759–1824), later Duchess of Devonshire. R.A. 1805 (195) : 250 × 144 : Ex Sir Vere Foster; A. M. Grenfell s. C. 26 June 1914 (48); Sir Hugh Lane; National Gallery of Ireland, Dublin.

Engr. F. C. Lewis, 1828. *Repr.* Plate 57. Appendix II (58).

FOULIS, Mrs. J. R. *See* SYKES, Beatrice Hester Decima.

FOX, Charles James (1749–1806). (1) Farington, 4 November 1800, notes that Lawrence had painted a portrait of Fox at St. Ann's Hill. Appendix II (59). (2) Lord Macaulay in a letter, mentions a portrait of Fox by Lawrence in the Library at Holland House 'the worst ever painted of so eminent a man by so eminent an artist'. This portrait is no longer in the Ilchester collections. (3) Possibly studio : 75 × 62 : Lord Lilford 1938. A copy of Lawrence's portrait of Fox, by Simpson, was included in lot 79 of the Lawrence sale, 18 June 1831.

FRAAS, Gemma Susanna (1820–1891). *c.* 1822 : 76 × 63, unfinished : Mrs. Stewart Murray, Ashley Court.

FRANCIS, Emperor of Austria (1768–1835). 1818 : 269 × 178 : H.M. the Queen, Windsor Castle (Waterloo Chamber) : painted at Aix-la-Chapelle. *Exhib.* B.I. 1830 (18).

FRANKLAND, Sir Thomas, 6th Bt. (1750–1831). *c.* 1810–15 : 76 × 63 : Ex Sir J. Frankland, Bt. : Howard Young Galleries, N.Y. : Arthur J. Secor : Toledo Museum of Art. *Repr.* Toledo Museum of Art, *Cat. European Paintings* 1939.

FRANKLAND, Sir Robert, 7th Bt. (1784–1849). *c.* 1810–15 : 76 × 63 : Ex Sir J. Frankland, Bt. : Howard Young Galleries, N.Y.: Mr. and Mrs. Alfred G. Wilson, Detroit.

FRASER of Lovat, Mrs. Thomas (Charlotte Georgina Jerningham) (1800–1876), later Lady Lovat. *c.* 1823 : 127 × 102 : Ex Lord Lovat : Jacques Seligman, N.Y.: Charles Blythe, San Francisco. Appendix III (71).

FRASER, Mrs. Charles, of Castle Fraser (Jane Hay). *c.* 1817 : 76 × 63 : Ex Col. Mackenzie Fraser; Knoedler; George W. Elkins 1914; Philadelphia Museum of Art.

FREDERICK WILLIAM III, King of Prussia (1770–1840). 1814–1818 : 272 × 179 : H.M. the Queen, Windsor Castle (Waterloo Chamber). *Exhib.* B.I. 1830 (17). *Replica* : Berlin Schloss.

FRIES, Victor von.

1819 : unfinished, 76 × 63 : Ex Count August von Fries ; Knoedler ; Carll Tucker, N.Y. : painted in Vienna.

Repr. Gowan.

FRY, Miss Caroline (1787–1846), later Mrs. Wilson.

R.A. 1830 (114) : 72 × 61 : National Gallery, London.

Repr. National Gallery, *Illustrations British School*, 1936.

FULLERTON, The Misses.

Begun 1825 : unfinished : cut down to 155 × 144 : Ex Charles Tattershall Dodd s. C. 10 July 1897, (86) : Max Michaelis, 1913.

Repr. Cat. 2nd National Loan Exhibition, 1913–14. Appendix III (72).

FUSELI, Henry, R.A. (1741–1825).

1825 : 146 × 111 : Ex Lawrence s. C., 15 May 1830 (54), bt. Seguier for Sir Robert Peel : Peel Heirlooms s. R. & F. 10 May 1906 (254) : possibly Musée Bonnat, Bayonne.

Exhib. Birmingham, *Society of Artists*, 1830 (84) ; B.I. 1833 (30). *Repr.* Goldring.

The portrait included in the Lawrence sale was described as 'bust only finished'. It may have been finished for Peel by Seguier, and in that case the Bayonne portrait is probably the original. The provenance of the Bayonne portrait is not known by the Museum authorities.

GALLOWAY, Jane (Paget), Countess of (d. 1842).

Date unrecorded : 76 × 63, unfinished : Earl of Galloway. Appendix III (73).

GARDNER, Alan Hyde, 2nd Baron (1722–1815).

Finished 1811 : 99 × 73 : by family descent to Lady Fry, Oare House.

Engr. H. Cook 1832.

GATAKER, Thomas, of Mildenhall (1749–1844).

Before 1795 : 73 × 62 : Ex M. Leicester Swale Gataker, s. C. 20 December 1918 (145) : Gooden and Fox; Lady Lever Gallery, Port Sunlight.

Appendix I (32).

VON GENTZ, Baron Friedrich (1764–1832).

1818 : 77 × 62 : H.M. the Queen, Windsor Castle.

Exhib. B.I. 1830 (36), 1833 (31).

Replica : 76·5 × 65 : Prince Paul Metternich-Winneburg, Vienna, 1913.

GEORGE III (1738–1820).

R.A. 1792 (65) : 276 × 154 : St. Mary's Guild-hall, Coventry.

Engr : Half length only : W. Holl 1830. *Repr.* Plate 7.

Replicas : (i) H.M. the Queen, Windsor Castle (Waterloo Chamber); (ii) the Earl of Dart-mouth, Patshull; (iii) The Town Hall, Liverpool (1821).

On his appointment as Painter in Ordinary to the King in 1792 Lawrence continued to copy Reynolds' state portraits of King George III and Queen Charlotte for official residences and private patrons, and did, in fact, complete six pairs left unfinished by Reynolds. A list, now at Coutts Bank, quotes 22 portraits of the King completed between 1809 and 1812. These would almost certainly be studio work and may have been repetitions of Lawrence's R.A. 1792 portrait.

GEORGE IV (1762–1830).

(1) R.A. 1815 (65) : 251 × 155 : Marquess of Londonderry, Londonderry House : in military uniform. *Replica*. Col. Leicester-Warren, Tabley House.

(2) Possibly R.A. 1818 (61) : 251 × 155 : H.M. the Queen, Buckingham Palace.

Engr. T. Hodgetts 1829.

In garter Robes. It is uncertain which of the many versions of this portrait was actually exhibited at the R.A.

Replicas : (i) Commissioned by Pope Pius VII 1819, Pinacoteca Vaticana, Rome; *Repr.* Plate 87; (ii) Marquess Conyngham, Slane Castle. *Repetitions* (i), (ii), (iii), H.M. the Queen, Windsor Castle (Waterloo Chamber, Throne Room and St. George's Hall); (iv) Formerly Royal House of Hanover; (v) Formerly Imperial Collection, St. Petersburg; (vi) Duke of Devonshire, Chatsworth; (vii) Marquess of Londonderry, Wynyard Park; (viii) Ex Lawrence s. C. 18 June 1831 (149) : the Athenaeum Club : presented by the Committee of the Athenaeum to the Corporation of Brighton, 1858; (ix) Drapers' Hall, London : commissioned 1826; (x) Town Hall, Windsor. Many other repetitions exist. The 6th Duke of Devonshire wrote in his *Handbook to Chatsworth* 1845, 'I accompanied William IV one day to Kensington Palace and found a room full of them' (i.e. portraits of George IV from the Lawrence studio).

Variant : Doctor's cap in place of Crown on table to left : 251 × 155 : the Examination Schools, Oxford.

(3) Finished November 1821. Probably R.A. 1822 (77) : 290 × 201 : H.M. the Queen, St. James's Palace : in Coronation Robes.

(4) Sitting July 1822 : 265 × 175 : Ex the Duchess of Teck : the Wallace Collection : In private dress.
Engr. C. Turner 1824. *Repr.* Plate 95.
Repetitions : Full-length : the Corporation of Brighton; *Three-quarter length* : (i) Duke of Devonshire, Chatsworth; (ii) Mr. & Mrs. Booth Tarkington, Indianapolis, 1941; (iii) Col. the Hon. John Fremantle, Wistow Hall; *Head and shoulders* : Ex Sir William Knighton : Scottish National Portrait Gallery. Many other repetitions exist.
(5) *c.* 1820 : 69 × 62 : said to have come from Woodburn and possibly identical with Lot 422, Lawrence sale C. 18 June 1830, bt. Woodburn : National Portrait Gallery.
Said to have been painted for the Coinage.
(6) '¾ portrait, the original head from which all the State pictures were painted' : Ex Lawrence s. C. 18 June 1831 (148), bt. General Grosvenor : Mrs. Grosvenor, 1856.
GÉRARD, François, Baron (1770–1837).
1825 : 76 × 63, unfinished : Palais de Versailles.
Repr. Plate 107.
GILMOR, Robert, junr. (1774–1848).
1818 : 76 × 63 : Robert Gilmor, junr., N.Y.
Engr. John Sartain. *Repr.* Plate 78.
GILMOR, Mrs. Robert, junr. (Sarah Reeves Ladson).
1818 : 76 × 63 : Mrs. Robert Gilmor, senr., N.Y.
Engr. John Sartain. *Repr.* Plate 79.
GLENBERVIE, Sylvester, Lord.
See DOUGLAS, Rt. Hon. Sylvester.
GLENGALL, Emily (Jefferys), Countess of (1767–1836).
1804 : 76 × 63, unfinished : Earl Stanhope, Chevening. Three heads on one canvas.
Repr. Gower.
GLOUCESTER, H.R.H. Princess Mary, Duchess of (1776–1857).
(1) R.A. 1817 (72) : 91 × 71 : Ex W. Dacres Adams : Major David Fisher-Rowe.
(2) R.A. 1824 (59) : 141 × 113 : H.M. the Queen, Windsor Castle.
GLOUCESTER, Bishop of.
See HUNTINGFORD, Dr. George Isaac.
GODERICH, Frederick John, Viscount.
See ROBINSON, Hon. Frederick John.
GODERICH, Sarah Albinia, Viscountess.
See ROBINSON, Lady Sarah.
GORDON, George, 5th Duke of (1770–1836).
c. 1825 : unfinished full-length : untraced.
Appendix III (77).

GORDON, Lady Georgiana (d. 1853), later Duchess of Bedford.
Sitting 1802 : unfinished : possibly identical with property of a gentleman, 58 × 48 : s. C. 13 July 1901 (104).
Exhib. B.I. 1830 (29), 1833 (43) : lent Duke of Bedford.
GORDON, Jane (Christie), Duchess of (*c.* 1780–1824).
c. 1810–15 : 142 × 112 : Ex Mrs. Cumming, Pembroke, 1909.
GORDON, Lady Louisa (d. 1850), later Marchioness Cornwallis.
R.A. 1795 (175) : 91 × 71 : Lord Braybrooke, Audley End.
GORDON, Lady William (Hon. Frances Ingram-Shepherd) (1761–1841).
c. 1806 : 91 × 71 : Ex Sir J. Ramsden s. C. 27 May 1932 (88).
Appendix II (62), Appendix III (76).
GORING, Mrs. Charles, of Wiston (Elizabeth Luxford) (d. 1811).
Payment 1809 : unfinished : untraced.
Appendix III (78).
GOTT, Benjamin (1762–1840).
c. 1827 : 140 × 114 : Mrs. P. M. Gott (on loan City Art Gallery, Leeds.)
GOTT, Mrs. Benjamin (Elizabeth Rhodes) (d. 1857).
1827 : 140 × 114 : Mrs. P. M. Gott (on loan City Art Gallery, Leeds). *Repr.* Plate 105.
GOWER, Harriet (Howard), Countess (1806–1868), later Duchess of Sutherland, and her daughter Elizabeth (d. 1878), later Duchess of Argyll.
R.A. 1828 (114) : 244 × 152 : Duke of Sutherland, Dunrobin Castle.
Mezz. S. Cousins, 1832. *Exhib.* B.I. 1830 (26).
GRAFTON, George Henry Fitzroy, 4th Duke of, K.G. (1760–1844).
Begun 1816 : 239 × 146 : Trinity College, Cambridge : finished by Simpson.
Appendix III (79).
GRAHAM, Lieut-Gen. Sir Thomas.
See LYNEDOCH, Lord.
GRANT, Sir William (1752–1832).
(1) R.A. 1802 (621) : 74 × 62 : Ex W. J. A. Grant of Hillersden s. C. 19 March 1948 (94) : Col. Mackenzie Smith.
Replica : 76 × 63 : Guildhall, London.
(2) R.A. 1820 (171) : 237 × 146 : National Portrait Gallery.
Engr. R. Golding. *Exhib.* B.I. 1830 (42).
GRANT, Mrs.
1801 : unfinished : untraced.
Appendix II (63), Appendix III (80).

CATALOGUE

GRANTHAM, Thomas Philip, 3rd Baron (1781–1859), later Earl de Grey.
Before 1806 : 76 × 63 : Lady Lucas, Woodyates Manor.
Appendix II (64).

GRANTHAM, Henrietta Frances (Cole), Lady (1784–1848), later Countess de Grey.
As Psyche.
R.A. 1814 (138) : 76 × 63 : Lady Lucas, Woodyates Manor.
Engr. J. H. Robinson 1828. *Exhib.* B.I. 1830 (30).

GRANVILLE, 1st Earl.
See LEVESON-GOWER, Lord Granville.

GREENWOOD, Charles (1748–1832).
Probably after 1815 : 127 × 102 : Captain H. C. Hammersley, Somerford Keynes.
Mezz. C. Turner 1828.

GREGG, Mrs. Francis, and her son George.
Before 1806 : 127 × 102 : Ex Mrs. C. V. Norman; Stanley Sedgwick; Mrs. Thomas J. Emery; Cincinnati Art Museum.
Possibly to be identified with *Mrs. Grigg*.
Appendix II (67).

GREVILLE, Lady Charlotte.
See BENTINCK, Lady Charlotte.

GREY, General Sir Charles of Falloden (1729–1807), later 1st Earl Grey.
R.A. 1795 (131) : 127 × 102 : Earl Grey, Howick.
Engr. J. Collyer 1797. *Repr.* Plate 28.

GREY, Charles, 2nd Earl (1764–1845).
(1) As Hon. C. Grey.
R.A. 1793 (614) : 127 × 102 : Earl Grey, Howick.
Mezz. W. Dickinson 1794. *Repr.* G. M. Trevelyan, *Lord Grey of the Reform Bill*, 1920.
(2) R.A. 1805 (96) : untraced.
Appendix II (65).
(3) As Earl Grey.
R.A. 1828 (158) : 127 × 102 : Earl Grey.
Mezz. S. Cousins 1830. *Repr.* G. M. Trevelyan, *Lord Grey of the Reform Bill*, 1920.

GREY, Mary Elizabeth (Ponsonby), Countess (1776–1831).
(1) With her daughters, Louisa (d. 1814), later Countess of Durham, and Elizabeth (d. 1843), later Mrs. Bulteel.
c. 1805 : circular, diam. 123 : Earl Grey, Howick.
Mezz. S. Cousins 1831.
Appendix II (66).
(2) R.A. 1813 (139) : 220 × 145 : Formerly Earl Grey, Howick : destroyed by fire.

Repr. G. M. Trevelyan, *Lord Grey of the Reform Bill*, 1920.

GRIFFITH, John, of the East India Co.
c. 1800 : 76 × 63 : Ex Rev. C. H. Cooke s. C. 20 May 1927 (166); Knoedler; John W. Sherwood, Baltimore.

GROTE, Mrs. George (Selina Mary Leckwell) (1775–1845).
c. 1800 : 127 × 102 : Ex Miss Mayor s. C. 20 May 1927 (33) : Messrs. P. & D. Colnaghi, London, 1952.

GUILFORD, Francis North, 4th Earl of (1761–1817).
(1) *c.* 1805–10 : 127 × 102 : Ex Henry North, 3rd Earl of Sheffield s. C. 11 December 1909 (103); possibly identical with Exors. of Gertrude Rogers s. P-B, N.Y., 26 November 1943.
(2) *c.* 1805–10 : 76 × 63 : head and shoulders similar to (1) : 3rd Earl of Sheffield s. C. 11 December 1909 (102) : M. C. Brunner, Paris, 1913.
Repr. Gowan.

GUILFORD, Susan (Coutts), Countess of (1771–1837).
(1) With her daughter Lady Georgiana North (d. 1835).
c. 1812 : 239 × 145 : Ex Lord North s. C. 11 July 1930 (80).
(2) Payment 1829 : unfinished half-length : untraced.
Appendix III (81).

GUNMAN, Mrs. James.
See DELAVAL, Sarah Hussey.

HALDIMAND, Anthony (1741–1817).
Before 1800 : 127 × 102 : Ex Sir P. Malcolm Stewart : the National Trust.

HALFORD, Sir Henry, Bt., M.P. (1766–1844).
After 1820 : 140 × 114 : Royal College of Physicians.
Mezz. C. Turner, 1830. *Repr. The Connoisseur*, July 1929.

HALKETT, Mrs. John (Anne Todd) (d. 1805).
c. 1802 : 236 × 145 : Ex Miss Madeline Halkett s. S. 27 February 1952 (12).
Appendix II (68).

HAMILTON, James, Viscount (1786–1814).
R.A. 1790 (219) : oval 51 × 40 : Duke of Abercorn, London.
Repr. Plate 12.
Probably Appendix I (1).

HAMILTON, Lord Claude (1787–1808).
c. 1792 : oval 51 × 40 : Duke of Abercorn, London.
Probably Appendix I (34).

HAMILTON, Lady Catherine.
See ABERDEEN, Catherine Elizabeth, Countess of.

HAMILTON, Lady Harriet (1781–1803).
(1) R.A. 1790 (275) : oval 51 × 40 : Duke of Abercorn, London.
(2) *c*. 1802 : 75 × 62 : Duke of Abercorn, London.
Repr. Gower.

HAMILTON, Lady Maria (1785–1814).
c. 1802 : 74 × 62 : Duke of Abercorn, London.
Repr. Gower.

HAMILTON, Emma (Hart), Lady (1761?–1815).
(1) As La Penserosa.
R.A. 1792 (i) : 239 × 146 : Marquess of Hamilton, Barons Court.
(2) As A Bacchante.
1792 : oval within a wreath of flowers by Jean Baptiste Mennoyer (1636–1699) : 165 × 118 : Countess Mountbatten, Broadlands.
The original centre, a Roman subject piece, was painted out in 1790 by Reynolds, who substituted a hand with an eye in it, emblem of Liberality guilded by Sagacity. Lawrence painted the head of Lady Hamilton over this emblem.
Repr. Gower.

HAMILTON, Dr.
Two portraits of 'Dr. Hamilton', 'Finished', were delivered to Mr. Fitzhugh, 1830/31.
Appendix III (82).

HAMOND, Sir Andrew Snape, 1st Bt. (1738–1828).
Before 1806 : 76 × 63 : Sir Egerton Hamond-Graeme, Bt., London.
Mezz. G. H. Phillips 1830. *Repr*. Plate 38.
Appendix II (71).

HAMOND, Fanny (1805–1819) and Jane (b. 1806) later Marchesa Bacella.
Sitting 1817 : 92 × 82 : Ex C. 10 July 1897 (68); Sedelmeyer 1897; Whitney Collection, N.Y., 1913.
Repr. Gowan.

HAMPDEN, Jane Maria (Brown), Viscountess (d. *c*. 1833).
Probably *c*. 1820 : 53 × 48, unfinished : Major A. J. G. Hope, Luffness House.

HARBORD, Caroline (Hobart), Lady (d. 1850), later Lady Suffield.
Probably R.A. 1793 (545) : 127 × 102 : trustees of the eleventh Marquess of Lothian.
Repr. Plate 30.

HARCOURT, Edward Venables Vernon (1757–1847), Archbishop of York.
R.A. 1823 (28) : 236 × 145 : Lord Vernon, Sudbury Hall.
Engr. G. H. Phillips 1836.

HARCOURT, Lady Elizabeth (Bingham) (d. 1838).
Payment 1823 : unfinished full-length : Viscount Harcourt.
Appendix III (147).

HARDENBURG, Carl August, Prince von (1750–1822).
1818 : 144 × 113 : H.M. the Queen, Windsor Castle (Waterloo Chamber) : painted at Aix-la-Chapelle.
Exhib. B.I. 1830 (13).

HARDINGE, Charles Stewart (1822–1894), later 2nd Viscount Hardinge, and Arthur Edward (1828–1892).
1829 : unfinished : untraced.
Appendix III (83).

HARDWICKE, Philip Yorke, 3rd Earl of (1757–1834).
R.A. 1830 (312) : 143 × 112 : Hon. Mrs. Marten, Crichel House.
Mezz. W. Giller 1836.

HARDY, Sarah (1780–1808), later Mrs. Daniel Lysons, and Charlotte Savery (1782–1850), later Mrs. Price, daughters of Col. Carteret Hardy.
1801 : 126 × 101 : Ex Lysons sale, Bruton, Knowles & Co., Gloucester, 21 April 1887 (284) : C. Roth : C. T. D. Crews s. C. 1 July 1915 (105) : J. L. Severance : Museum of Art, Cleveland, U.S.A.

HARE, John.
Sitting 1800 : untraced.
Appendix II (73).

HAREWOOD, Henry Lascelles, 2nd Earl of (1767–1841).
R.A. 1823 (7) : 268 × 176 : Earl of Harewood, Harewood House.
Mezz. T. Lupton 1828. *Repr*. Borenius, *Cat. Pictures and Drawings Harewood House*, 1936.

HARFORD, John Scandrett (1785–1866).
c. 1824 : 76 × 63 : Sir Arthur Harford, Bt., Standen House.

HARFORD, Mrs. John Scandrett (Louisa Hart-Davis) (1796–1872).
R.A. 1824 (119) : 76 × 63 : Ex Harford Family : George Coats : Lord Glentanar.
Engr. W. H. Worthington 1827. *Exhib*. Bristol, Institution for Promotion of Literature, Science and the Fine Arts, 1826 : B.I. 1830 (22), 1833 (42). *Repr*. Gowan.

HART-DAVIS, Richard, M.P. (1766–1842).
R.A. 1815 (276) : 76 × 63 : Rupert Hart-Davis, London.
Engr. W. Sharp 1816.
Exhib. Bristol, Institution for Promotion of Literature, Science and the Arts, 1826; B.I. 1830 (45), 1833 (7).

S.T.L.—D

HART-DAVIS, Hart (1791–1854).
c. 1808–9 : 76 × 63 : Provost's Lodge, Eton College.
Repr. Cust, *Eton Portraits*, 1910.
Replica : 76 × 63 : Ex Rev. R. H. Hart-Davis s. C. 14 July 1922 (26) : private Collection, U.S.A. *Exhib.* B.I. 1833 (29).

HART-DAVIS, Mrs. Hart (Charlotte Dundas), (1790–1861).
After 1813 : 76 × 63 : Ex Rev. R. H. Hart-Davis s. C. 14 July, 1922 (25) : John Levy, N.Y. 1925 : Mr. A. H. Houghton; Mrs. John J. Campbell, III, N.Y.
Exhib. B.I. 1830 (23*), 1833 (1).

HARVEY, Sir Felton.
A portrait of Sir Felton Harvey was claimed by his widow from the executors of Lawrence. Appendix III (85).

HARVEY, Charles, M.D., F.R.S., F.S.A (1757–1843) (later adopted the surname Savile-Onley).
1804 : 243 × 112 : St. Andrew's Hall, Norwich. Appendix II (74).
Mezz. C. Turner 1820.

HARVEY, Lady Louisa (Nugent) (1758–1841), and her children, Edward (1788–1812), and Louisa (1785–1866), later Mrs. William Lloyd of Aston.
Begun 1793 : 244 × 144 : Andrew Lloyd, Lyndhurst.
Appendix II (79), Appendix III (84).

HASTINGS, Francis, Marquess of.
See RAWDON, Francis, Lord.

HASTINGS, Warren (1732–1818).
R.A. 1811 (194) : 90 × 70 : Ex J. P. Fearon : National Portrait Gallery.
Mezz. W. Say 1813. *Repr.* Plate 64.

HATHERTON, Hyacinthe Mary, Lady.
See LITTLETON, Hon. Mrs. John.

HAWKESBURY, Robert Lord.
See LIVERPOOL, 2nd Earl of.

HEALD, Sir George Trafford, K.C.
c. 1825 : 89 × 69 : untraced.
Repr. Armstrong.

HEATHCOTE, Sir Gilbert (1773–1851).
R.A. 1791 (385) : 76 × 63 : Earl of Ancaster, Grimsthorpe Castle.
Repr. Plate 17.
Appendix I (35).

HEMMING, Frederick H.
1824–5 : 76 × 63 : Ex Hemming s. C. 3 April 1881 (245) : Henry Seligman s. N.Y. 29 March 1934 (37) (repr. cat.) : Mrs. C. W. Dresselhuis, N.Y.

HEMMING, Mrs. F. H. (Miss Bloxam).
1824–5 : 75 × 62 : Ex Hemming s. C. 13 April 1881 (246) : Adolphe Hirsch 1913 : Thomas Manville : Mrs. C. W. Dresselhuis, N.Y.
Exhib. Birmingham, Institution for Promoting the Fine Arts, 1828 (78). *Repr.* Armstrong.

HENRY, John Joseph (d. 1835).
Before 1806 : 75 × 62 : by family descent to Mrs. Barbara Armstrong, Gyfelia.
Appendix II (77).

HERTFORD, Francis Charles Seymour, 3rd Marquess of (1777–1842).
c. 1825 : 127 × 101 : Ex Sir J. Murray Scott s. C. 27 June 1913 (109) : Blakeslee sale, N.Y., April 1915.
Engr. W. Holl 1833.

HIBBERT, George, M.P. (1757–1837).
1811 : 243 × 112 : Port of London Authority.

HILL, Lord Marcus (1798–1863), later Lord Sandys.
c. 1820 : 76 × 63 : Lord Sandys, Ombersley Court.
Engr. W. Skelton.

HILLYER, Mrs.
c. 1795 : 76 × 63 : Ex Agnew 1913; Sir Otto Beit, Bt.; Mrs. Arthur Bull.

HINCHINBROOKE, Louisa (Lowry-Corry) Lady (1781–1862), later Countess of Sandwich.
Payment 1804 : 240 × 145 : Earl of Sandwich, Hinchinbrooke.
Repr. Country Life, 13 April 1929.
Appendix II (80), Appendix III (133).

HOARE, Henry, of Mitcham Grove (1750–1828).
R.A. 1805 (157) : 127 × 102 : formerly at Killerton : painted for Sir Thomas Dyke Acland, Bt.
Engr. H. Meyer.

HOARE, Prince (1755–1834).
c. 1826 : 61 × 51 : unfinished : Ex W. Hookham Carpenter s. C. 16 February 1867 (17) : anon. s. C. 21 February 1919 (88).
Mezz. C. Turner 1831.
Appendix III (86).

HOBART, Lady Amelia Anne.
See LONDONDERRY, Amelia Anne, Marchioness of.

HOOD, Hon. Mary (Mackenzie), Lady (1783–1862), later Mrs. Stewart Mackenzie.
R.A. 1808 (133) : 236 × 146 : Marquess of Northampton, Castle Ashby.
Mezz. S. W. Reynolds. *Exhib.* B.I. 1830 (24).

HOPE, Henry Philip (d. 1839).
Sitting *c.* 1805 : 256 × 177 : Ex Hope Heirlooms s. C. 20 July 1917 (63), bt. Tata.
Appendix II (81), Appendix III (87).

HOPE, Hon. Mrs. Thomas (Hon. Louisa Beresford) (d. 1851), later Viscountess Beresford.
R.A. 1826 (158) : 75 × 62 : Ex Hope heirlooms s. C. 20 July 1917 (62) : Knoedler : D. G. Reid, U.S.A., 1918.
Engr. E. Scriven 1830. *Exhib*. B.I. 1830 (27).

HOPE, Charles (died young).
As the infant Bacchus.
1816 : Circular diam. 63 : Ex Hope Heirlooms s. C. 20 July 1917 (64) : Duke of Newcastle.
Mezz. S. Cousins 1836. *Exhib*. B.I. 1830 (28).

HOPE, Gen. the Hon. Alexander (1769–1837).
1810 : 76 × 63 : Marquess of Linlithgow, London.
Engr. W. Walker 1825.

HOPE, Georgiana (Brown), Lady (d. 1855).
c. 1805 : 76 × 63 : Major A. J. G. Hope, Luffness.

HORNBY, Lady Charlotte (Stanley) (1776–1805).
c. 1795 : 76 × 63 : Earl of Derby, Knowsley Hall.
Probably Appendix I (37).

HOUSTON, Lady Jane.
See LONG, Lady Jane.

HOWDEN, John, Baron.
See CRADOCK, Lieut.-Gen. Sir John.

HOWLEY, William (1766–1848), Bishop of London, later Archbishop of Canterbury.
R.A. 1816 (25) : 142 × 112 : Winchester College.
Mezz. C. Turner 1817.

HUMBOLDT, Karl Wilhelm, Baron von (1767–1835).
c. 1820 : 133 × 105 : H.M. the Queen, Windsor Castle (Waterloo Chamber) : head only by Lawrence, finished by Evans.

HUNTER, John, of Gobions (*c*. 1724–1802).
(1) Possibly R.A. 1789 (130) : 127 × 102 : Ex anon. s. C. 11 February 1911 (83) : H. I. Pratt, N.Y. : Wildenstein, N.Y.
Appendix I (38).
(2) *c*. 1790 : 127 × 102 : Ex Rev. G. S. Little s. C. 25 July 1913 (145) : R. B. Pyne, jr. : Scott and Fowles, N.Y.

HUNTINGFORD, Dr. George Isaac (1748–1832), Bishop of Gloucester, later Bishop of Hereford.
R.A. 1805 (219) : 142 × 112 : Winchester College.
Mezz. James Ward 1807.

HUNTLY, Elizabeth, Marchioness of.
See CONYNGHAM, Lady Elizabeth.

HUSKISSON, William, M.P. (1770–1830).
Finished 1829 : 76 × 63 : Ex Peel Heirlooms s. R. & F. 29 November 1917 (81) : The Earl of Harewood, Harewood House.
Engr. W. Finden 1831. *Exhib*. B.I. 1833 (24). Appendix III (88).

IMPEY, Hastings (1782–1805).
c. 1798 : oval 76 × 63 : Major Edward Impey, Lymington.

IMPEY, Edward (1785–1858).
c. 1798 : oval 76 × 63 : Major Edward Impey, Lymington.

INCHBALD, Mrs. Samuel (Elizabeth Simpson) (1753–1821).
1796 : 76 × 63, unfinished : H. M. Adams, Cambridge.
Engr. S. Freeman 1807.

INCHIQUIN, Murrough O'Brian, 5th Earl of (1724?–1808), later 1st Marquess of Thomond.
R.A. 1797 (148) : 143 × 107 : National Gallery of Ireland, Dublin.

INCHIQUIN, Mary (Palmer), Countess of (1751–1802), later Marchioness of Thomond.
(1) R.A. 1795 (175) : 92 × 71 : Ex Lady Colomb : T. G. M. Snagge, London.
Engr. W. Bond. *Repr*. Gower.
(2) *c*. 1800 : 80 × 69, unfinished : Ex anon. s. C. February 1903 : The Louvre. Perhaps Appendix III (144); but as this portrait appeared in the sale room as *Mrs. Siddons*, was exhibited in 1905 as *Mrs. Forster*, and is catalogued by the Louvre as *Countess of Inchiquin* the identity of the sitter seems to be in doubt.

INGESTRE, Sarah Elizabeth (Beresford), Lady (1807–1884).
c. 1828 : 236 × 145, unfinished : Earl of Shrewsbury, Ingestre.
Appendix III (89).

JEBB, Dr. John, Bishop of Limerick (1775–1833).
1826 : 91 × 71 : untraced.
Mezz. T. Lupton 1830.

JEKYLL, Joseph, M.P., F.R.S. (1752–1837).
R.A. 1817 (346) : 76 × 63 : by family descent to Lady Freyberg, London.
Mezz. W. Say 1818. *Repr. The Farington Diary*, ed. Grieg, 1923, Vol. VIII.

JENNER, Edward, M.D., F.R.S. (1749–1823).
c. 1809 : 76 × 63 : Ex Miss Baron of Cheltenham.
Repetition : 76 × 63 : Ex Dr. Baron : W. H. Bailie : Royal College of Physicians.
Lith. J. H. Lynch.

JENNINGS, Elizabeth, later Mrs. William Lock, II.
R.A. 1799 (223) : full-length : Ex Lord Wallscourt : Agnew 1912.

Repr. Gowan.

Replica : Head and shoulders only : oval 76 × 63 : Duchess of Sermoneta, Rome.

Repr. Gower.

Repetition : (1) Half-length only : 127 × 102 : Viscount Kemsley, London; (ii) Half-length only : 127 × 102 : Ex Mrs. B. F. Jones, Pittsburgh : Mrs. C. W. Dressellhuis, N.Y.

JERSEY, George Child Villiers, 5th Earl of (1773–1859).

Begun 1815 : 249 × 146 : formerly Earl of Jersey : destroyed by fire 1950 : finished by J. Simpson.

Appendix III (90).

JERSEY, Sarah Sophia (Fane), Countess of (1785–1867).

R.A. 1823 (89) : 236 × 144 : formerly Earl of Jersey : destroyed by fire 1950.

Repr. Armstrong.

JERSEY, Julia, Countess of.

See PEEL, Julia.

JOHNSTONE, Mrs. (1756–1813), afterwards Mrs. (later Lady) Nugent.

1789 : 76 × 63 : H. J. R. Bankes, Kingston Lacy. Possibly Appendix I (39). Possibly also identical with Appendix I (62).

JOLIFFE, Thomas Samuel, M.P. (1746–1824).

1822 : 127 × 102 : Lord Hylton, Ammerdown.

JONES, Mrs. Robert Burnet (Elizabeth Susannah Eastwicke) (d. 1843).

Possibly R.A. 1794 (168) : 76 × 63 : Ex anon. (Jones Family) s. C. 7 May 1909 (72) : Barnet Lewis s. C. 28 February 1930 (99), (repr. cat.) : Mrs. F. H. Cook, Guildford.

JONES, Sir Richard.

1827 : unfinished : untraced.

Appendix III (91).

KAYE, Dr. John (1783–1853).

Payment 1828 : 127 × 102 : The Old Palace, Lincoln : finished by Say.

Appendix III (98).

KELLY, Michael (1764?–1826).

Before 1795 : 76 × 63 : untraced.

Engr. J. Neagle 1798.

Appendix I (40).

KEMBLE, Mrs. Roger (Sarah Ward) (1735–1807).

c. 1800 : 76 × 63 : by family descent to Alice, Lady Butler, London.

Engr. S. Freeman 1808. *Repr.* Plate 42.

KEMBLE, John Philip (1757–1823).

(1) Possibly R.A. 1797 (188) : 76 × 63 : by family descent to C. K. B. Wister, Haverford, Pa.

Repr. Pennsylvania Museum Bulletin, February 1924.

(2) As *Coriolanus*.

R.A. 1798 (225) : 287 × 178 : Ex Sir Richard Worsley : Earl of Yarborough, by whom presented to the Guildhall Art Gallery, 1906.

Engr. R. M. Meadows 1805. *Repr.* Plate 36.

(3) As *Rolla*.

R.A. 1800 (193) : 335 × 223 : Ex Sir Robert Peel : Peel Heirlooms s. R. & F. 10/11 May 1900 (214), bt. Robson.

Mezz. S. W. Reynolds 1803. *Exhib.* B.I. 1806.

(4) As *Hamlet*.

R.A. 1801 (197) : 305 × 198 : Ex Maddocks, M.P. s. European Museum, St. James's, 1812 : Robert Ashby : T. Lawrence : George IV, by whom purchased from Lawrence : William IV, by whom presented to the National Gallery, 1836 : the Tate Gallery.

Mezz. S. W. Reynolds 1805. *Repr.* Plate 48. *Exhib.* B.I. 1825 (96), 1830 (87), 1833 (19).

Replicas : (1) small version : Ex Sir Thomas Baring s. C. 2 June 1848 (46). *Exhib.* B.I. 1830 (33). (ii) Head and shoulders only : 76 × 63 : presented by Lawrence to Miss Harriet Lee : the late W. H. Lee Ewart, Mont-au-Prêtre.

Repetitions : (i) *c.* 161 × 109 : by family descent to C. K. B. Wister, Haverford, Pa. ; (ii) 183 × 112 : Ex J. Orrock s. C. 6 June 1904 (270) : Lord Leverhulme s. Anderson Galls, N.Y., 17/19 February 1926 (156) : Folger Shakespeare Library, Washington. Other repetitions exist.

(5) Possibly R.A. 1804 (110) : 142 × 112 : Ex Property of a nobleman s. C. 13 July 1895 (55) : Francis J. Bartlett, U.S.A. : Museum of Fine Arts, Boston.

Mezz. W. Say 1814.

Perhaps identical with the portrait, 144 × 112, lent by Col. North to the Manchester Art Treasures Exhibition, 1857.

(6) Possibly R.A. 1804 (110) : 76 × 63 : Ex Rowland Stephenson 1826.

Engr. C. Turner, for Boaden's *Kemble*, 1826.

(7) As *Cato*.

R.A. 1812 (57) : size unrecorded : Ex Lord Blessington 1831.

Engr. W. Ward. *Exhib.* Birmingham, Society of Artists, 1829 (1); B.I. 1830 (67).

Appendix III (92).

Replica : 89 × 74 : painted for Charles Mathews : Garrick Club, London.

KENYON, George Kenyon, 2nd Baron (1776–1855).

1805–9 : 75 × 62 : Lord Kenyon, Gredington.

KNIGHT, Richard Payne, M.P. (1750–1824).

(1) R.A. 1794 (181) : 127 × 102 : Major W. M. P. Kincaid-Lennox, Downton Castle. *Repr.* Plate 29.

(2) 1805 : 93 × 61 : Society of Dilettanti, London. *Mezz.* J. Bromley.

KNIGHT, Mrs. Samuel (Spelman), (d. 1800). Before 1800 : unfinished, 76 × 63 : by family descent to R. B. Beart.

KNIGHTON, Sir William, Bt., M.D. (1776–1836). R.A. 1823 (318) : 127 × 102 : by family descent to G. Stanley Hawker, M.P., South Australia. *Mezz.* C. Turner.

KNIGHTON, Dorothea (Hawker), Lady. 1827 : unfinished : untraced. Appendix III (93).

KYNNERSLEY, Mrs. Clement (Rosamund Dixie). Before 1800 : 75 × 62 : Ex Charles Bowyer Adderley, Hams Hall : prop. nobleman s. C. 16 June 1911 (131) : Norman Forbes-Robertson (1913) : Speyer s. P-B., N.Y., 10/11 April 1942 (23).

LABOUCHÈRE, Henry (1798–1869), later 1st Lord Taunton, and John (1799–1863), sons of Peter Caesar Labouchère. R.A. 1811 (70) : *c.* 238 × 142 : Ex Lord Taunton : Henry Reinhardt and Sons, N.Y., 1924. *Engr.* C. W. Wass.

LAMB, Hon. William (1779–1848), later 2nd Viscount Melbourne.
(1) *c.* 1805–10 : 76 × 63 : Cowper Collection, Panshanger. *Engr.* S. Freeman 1832.
(2) *c.* 1805–10 : 76 × 62 : Dowager Viscountess Hambleden. *Repr.* Plate 53.

LAMB, Lady Caroline (Ponsonby) (1785–1828). 1809 : 53 × 47 : Ex Claude Ponsonby s. C. 28 March 1908 (22) : George F. de Menasce : City Art Gallery, Bristol : much restored. Appendix III (94).

LAMB, Hon. Emily (1787–1869), later (1) Countess Cowper, (2) Lady Palmerston.
(1) With her sister Harriet. R.A. 1792 (513) : 75 × 63 : Cowper Collection, Panshanger. *Repr.* Plate 11. Appendix I (51).
(2) R.A. 1803 (127) : 76 × 63 : Cowper Collection, Panshanger. *Repr.* Plate 54. *Exhib.* B.I. 1830 (39). *Repetition* : 50 × 41 : Countess Mountbatten of Burma, Broadlands.

LAMBTON, John George, M.P. (1792–1840), later 1st Earl of Durham.

R.A. 1829 (135) : 76 × 63 : Earl of Durham. *Mezz.* C. Turner, 1831. *Exhib.* B.I. 1830 (51), 1833 (39). *Repr.* Plate 94.

LAMBTON, Lady Louisa (Grey) (1797–1841), later Countess of Durham. R.A. 1821 (180) : 239 × 146 : Earl of Durham. *Mezz.* S. Cousins. *Exhib.* B.I. 1825 (48).

LAMBTON, Charles William (1818–1831). R.A. 1825 (288) : 141 × 110 : Earl of Durham. *Mezz.* S. Cousins, 1827. *Exhib.* B.I. 1830 (49). *Repr.* Plate 98.

LANE-FOX, Mrs. George (Georgiana Henrietta Buckley). 1829 : unfinished : untraced. Appendix III (70).

LANSDOWNE, Henry Petty Fitzmaurice, 3rd Marquess of (1780–1863). *c.* 1827 : 139 × 109 : Marquess of Lansdowne, Bowood : intended for a full length. *Mezz.* J. Bromley 1831. *Exhib.* B.I. 1830 (44).

LANSDOWNE, Louisa (Fox-Strangways), Marchioness of (d. 1851). 1825–6 : 107 × 81 : Marquess of Lansdowne, Bowood.

LASCELLES, Lady Louisa (1812–1886), later Lady George Cavendish. *c.* 1829 : oval 60 × 50, unfinished : Earl of Harewood, Harewood House. *Repr.* Borenius *Cat. Pictures and Drawings at Harewood House*, 1936. *Repetition* : 51 × 37 : Ex Thos. J. Barrett : Lord Leverhulme : Lady Lever Art Gallery, Port Sunlight.

LAUDERDALE, James Maitland, 8th Earl of (1759–1839). Before 1795 : untraced. Appendix I (41).

LAW, Ewan, M.P. (d. 1829). Before 1795 : 76 × 63 : untraced. Appendix I (42).

LAWLEY, Anna Maria (Denison), Lady (d. 1850). *c.* 1795 : 76 × 63, unfinished : Ex W. Dacres Adams : W. G. H. Rawlinson, London.

LAWRENCE, Sir Thomas, P.R.A. (1769–1830).
(1) *c.* 1786 : 58 × 49 : Ex John Meredith : C. R. Aston s. C. 3 July 1908 (141) : anon. s. C. 28 January 1911 (139). *Exhib.* B.I. 1830 (91).
(2) *c.* 1825 : 91 × 69, unfinished : Ex Lawrence s. C. 18 June 1831 (150) : Earl of Chesterfield : Royal Academy of Arts. *Mezz.* S. Cousins 1830. *Exhib.* B.I. 1833 (14). *Repr.* Plate 106.

LAWRENCE, Rev. Andrew (d. 1821).
(1) R.A. 1790 (260) : 75 × 62 : Ex anon. s. C. 8 April 1932 (125).
(2) 1804 : 127 × 102 : Ex anon. s. C. 17 February 1906 (85) : Christopher Norris s. C. 4 July 1952 (12).
Repr. Goldring.

LE BEAUVOIR, Sir T.
1827 : unfinished full length : untraced.
Appendix III (18).

LE BRETON, Sir Thomas (1763–1838).
c. 1825 : 124 × 99 : Pembroke College, Oxford.
Mezz. C. Turner 1827.

LEE, George Augustus.
Before 1806 : 76 × 63 : Ex Miss Harriet Lee : the late W. H. Lee Ewart, Mont-au-Prêtre.
Probably Appendix II (90).

LEEDS, Francis Godolphin, 5th Duke of (1751–1799).
R.A. 1796 (103) : 239 × 147 : Lady Diana Pelham, Brocklesby Park.
Engr. R. M. Meadows 1792.

LEGGE, Hon. William (1784–1853), later 4th Earl of Dartmouth.
c. 1802 : 69 × 58 : Provosts Lodge, Eton College.
Repr. Cust, *Eton Portraits*, 1910.

LEGH, Mrs. George John (Mary Blackburne).
Begun 1803 : 76 × 63, unfinished : Formerly C. L. S. Cornwall-Legh : destroyed by fire 1944.
Perhaps Appendix II (92), probably Appendix III (96).

LEICESTER, Thomas, Earl of.
See COKE, Thomas W., M.P.

LEICESTER, Georgina Mary (Cottin), Lady (1794–1859), later Lady de Tabley.
As *Hope*.
R.A. 1814 (56) : 239 × 144 : Lt.-Col. J. Leicester Warren, Tabley House.
Engr. H. Meyer 1823.

LEITRIM, Mary (Bermingham), Countess of (d. 1840), and her daughter Maria (d. 1885), later Mrs. Edward Keppel.
Payment before 1806 : 139 × 110 : Earl of Leitrim, Mulroy.
Repr. Commem. Cat. Exhibition British Art, Royal Academy, 1935.
Appendix II (93).

LENNOX, Lady Mary Louisa (1760–1843).
R.A. 1789 (232) : 76 × 63 : Earl Bathurst, Cirencester House.
Repr. Earl Bathurst, *Cat. Bathurst Coll.*, 1908.
Appendix I (43).

Variant : 76 × 63 : Earl Bathurst, Cirencester House.
Repr. Earl Bathurst, *Cat. Bathurst Coll.*, 1908.

LEOPOLD, H.R.H. Prince, of Saxe-Coburg (1790–1865).
1821 : 269 × 178 : H.M. the Queen, Windsor Castle (Waterloo Chamber).
Replica : H.M. the King of the Belgians.
Exhib. B.I. 1830 (34).

LEVESON-GOWER, Lord Francis (1800–1857), later Lord Francis Egerton, and 1st Earl of Ellesmere.
R.A. 1827 (212) : 76 × 63 : Duke of Sutherland, Sutton Place.

LEVESON-GOWER, Lady Elizabeth (1797–1891), later Viscountess Belgrave, and Marchioness of Westminster.
R.A. 1818 (53) : 76 × 63 : the Duke of Sutherland, Sutton Place.
Engr. J. Thompson 1825. *Repr. Les Arts*, January 1913.
Replica : The Duke of Norfolk, Arundel Castle.

LEVESON-GOWER, Lord Granville (1773–1846), later 1st Earl Granville.
c. 1795–8 : 239 × 145 : Earl Granville.
Repr. Plate 39.

LIBROMISKI, Child of Count.
1818 : sketch, ¾ length : untraced : painted in Vienna.

LIEVEN, Prince Christopher Andreievitch (1772–1839).
c. 1812–15 : 127 × 102 : H.S.H. Princess Lieven, 1937.
Repr. H. Montgomery Hyde, *Princess Lieven*, 1938.
Appendix III (97).

LIEVEN, Princess (Dorothea von Benckendorff) (1785–1857).
After 1812 : 46·5 × 38·5, unfinished : Ex Lawrence s. C. 18 June 1831 (75) : R. Winstanley s. C. 16 March 1850 (14) : Sir Robert Peel : The National Gallery : possibly cut down from an unfinished full-length.
Repr. Plate 81.

LINCOLN, Bishop of.
See KAYE, Dr. John.

LINLEY, William (1771–1835).
R.A. 1789 (171) : 75 × 62 : The Dulwich Gallery.
Mezz. T. Lupton, 1840. *Exhib.* B.I. 1833 (32).
Repr. Gower.

LITTLETON, Hon. Mrs. John (Hyacinthe Mary Wellesley) (d. 1849), later Lady Hatherton.
R.A. 1822 (67) : 91 × 71 : Lord Hatherton (1913).
Mezz. C. Turner 1827. *Exhib.* B.I. 1830 (48).

LIVERPOOL, Robert Banks Jenkinson, 2nd Earl of (1770–1828).
(1) As Lord Hawkesbury.
c. 1795 : 127 × 102 : untraced.
Mezz. Inigo Young 1801.
(2) *c.* 1800 : 76 × 63 : unfinished : Ex Col. C. J. C. Grant s. C. 11 May 1923 (109) : Major J. S. Courtauld s. C. 27 October 1938 (246) : Mrs. Henry Dreyfus.
(3) *c.* 1800 : 76 × 63 : Ex Lord Taunton; Walter de Zoete s. C. 5 April 1935 (93); Leggatt; Lord Faringdon, Buscot Park.
The identification with Lord Liverpool is uncertain.
(4) As Earl of Liverpool.
Payment before 1823 : 138 × 105 : H.M. the Queen, Windsor Castle.
Mezz. C. Turner, 1827. *Exhib.* B.I. 1830 (12).
(5) R.A. 1827 (117) : 234 × 142 : Ex Peel Heirlooms s. R. & F. 29/30 November 1917 (65) : National Portrait Gallery.
Exhib. B.I. 1830 (50).

LOCK, William (1), of Norbury Park (1732–1810).
R.A. 1790 (19) : 76 × 63 : Ex Trustees of W. Angerstein s. C. 4 July 1896 (114) : Denman Waldo Ross : Museum of Fine Arts, Boston.
Repr. Plate 22.
The Public Advertiser, 30 April 1790, described this portrait as executed at a single sitting.
Appendix I (44).
More finished versions of (1) in which the sitter appears older are (i) Ex Trustees of W. Angerstein s. C. 4 December 1897 (28), bt. in : by family descent to J. A. L. Smythies : *Repr.* Duchess of Sermoneta, *The Locks of Norbury*, 1940; (ii) Hon. Mrs. Leycester Storr.

LOCK, Mrs. William (1) (Federica Augusta Schaub) (1750–1832).
R.A. 1829 (455) : 76 × 63 : Ex Trustees of W. Angerstein s. C. 4 July 1896 (113), bt. in : by family descent to J. A. L. Smythies.
Repr. Plate III.

LOCK, William (2) (1767–1847).
R.A. 1791 (140) : 76 × 63 : untraced.
Appendix I (45).

LOCK, Mrs. William (2).
See JENNINGS, Elizabeth.

LOCK, William (3) (1804–1832).
R.A. 1814 (277) : 127 × 102 : Ex Lord

Wallscourt : Sir J. B. Robinson s. C. 6 July 1923 (16), bt. Amor.
Engr. W. Humphrys, 1828, for *The Bijou*.

LOCK, Charles (1770–1804).
c. 1795–1800 : 76 × 63 : untraced.
A version of this portrait, possibly the original, was at one time in the Kann Collection, Paris.

LOCK, Mrs. Charles (Cecilia Ogilvie) (1775–1824).
R.A. 1797 (237) : probably 76 × 63 : untraced.
Farington records, 26 February 1796, that Lawrence had undertaken 'to paint a picture containing two whole lengths of Mrs. Charles Lock (late Miss Ogilvie) and her sister Miss Ogilvie'. This project appears to have been abandoned for two half-length portraits.

LOCKHART, Mrs. William (Sarah Jane Pelliser).
Begun 1826 : 76 × 63, unfinished : Stephen Lockhart, London.
Appendix III (99).

LOMAX, Mrs.
Begun 1826 : unfinished : untraced.
Appendix III (100).

LONDON, Bishop of.
See HOWLEY, William.

LONDONDERRY, Robert Stewart, 2nd Marquess of (1769–1822).
As Viscount Castlereagh.
(1) R.A. 1794 (131) : 127 × 102 : Marquess of Londonderry, Wynyard Park.
Repr. H. M. Hyde, *Londonderry House and its Pictures*, 1937.
(2) R.A. 1810 (61) : 74 × 61 : Ex 2nd Earl of Clancarty to whom presented by sitter : Earl of Clancarty s. C. 12 March 1892 (48) : National Portrait Gallery.
Engr. H. Meyer 1814. *Repr.* Plate 61.
(3) R.A. 1814 (23) : 127 × 102 : Marquess of Londonderry, Londonderry House.
Mezz. C. Turner 1814. *Repr.* H. M. Hyde, *Londonderry House and its Pictures*, 1937.
Star and Ribbon of the Garter added 1815/16.
Repetitions : (i) H.M. the Queen, Windsor Castle, (Waterloo Chamber), *exhib.* B.I. 1830 (16); (ii) G. P. Holford to whom given by sitter : Sir G. Holford s. C. 18 May 1928 (109) : Mrs. G. Rasmussen s. C. 25 February 1938 (71) : Marquess of Londonderry, Mount Stewart; (iii) Earl of Clanwilliam, London.
(4) As Marquess of Londonderry.
1821 : 287 × 193 : Marquess of Londonderry, Wynyard Park.
Mezz. C. Turner, 1822. *Repr.* H. M. Hyde, *Londonderry House and its Pictures*, 1937.

LONDONDERRY, Amelia Anne (Hobart), Marchioness of (1772–1829).
(1) R.A. 1794 (168) : 125 × 99 : Marquess of Londonderry, Londonderry House.
Repr. H. M. Hyde, *Londonderry House and its Pictures*, 1937.
Repetitions : (i) The National Trust, Blickling Hall; (ii) Marquess of Londonderry, Mount Stewart.
(2) As Marchioness of Londonderry.
c. 1825 : 76 × 63 : untraced.
Engr. J. Thomson 1826.
(3) *c.* 1825–30 : 220 × 145 : Marquess of Londonderry, Wynyard Park.
Possibly Appendix III (101).

LONDONDERRY, Charles, 3rd Marquess of.
See STEWART, Lord Charles.

LONDONDERRY, Frances Anne (Tempest), Marchioness of (1800–1865).
(1) 1819 : 76 × 63 : Marquess of Londonderry, London : painted in Vienna.
Engr. J. Cochran 1826. *Exhib.* B.I. 1830 (70).
Repr. H. M. Hyde, *Londonderry House and its Pictures*, 1937.
Repetition : 76 × 63 : Ex Marchioness of Londonderry s. C. 23 February 1907 (129) : Oscar Cintas, Havana.
(2) With her son, George Henry, Viscount Seaham.
R.A. 1828 (140) : 254 × 152 : Marquess of Londonderry, Wynyard Park.
Engr. C. Rolls 1832. *Exhib.* B.I. 1830 (75).

LONDONDERRY, Frederick, 4th Marquess of.
See STEWART, Hon. Frederick.

LONDONDERRY, George Henry, 5th Marquess of.
See SEAHAM, George Henry, Viscount.

LONG, Lady Jane (Maitland), later Lady Houston (d. 1833).
R.A. 1796 (102) : 76 × 63 : Ex Hon. Mrs. Hugh Elliot s. S. 13 February 1935 (134) : Messrs T. Agnew 1952.
Appendix I (47).

LONSDALE, William, 1st Earl of, K.G. (1757–1844).
R.A. 1812 (19) : 127 × 102 : Earl of Lonsdale, Penrith.
Mezz. C. Turner.

LONSDALE, Augusta (Fane) Countess of (d. 1838).
Payment 1817 : 91 × 71 : Earl of Lonsdale, Penrith.
Appendix III (102).

LOTHIAN, John William Robert, 7th Marquess of (1794–1841).

c. 1824 : 92 × 71, unfinished : trustees of the eleventh Marquess of Lothian.
Appendix III (104).

LOVAT, Charlotte, Lady.
See FRASER OF LOVAT, Mrs.

LOWTHER, Col. the Hon. Henry Cecil (1790–1867).
R.A. 1818 (284) : 127 × 102 : Earl of Lonsdale, Penrith.
Mezz. G. H. Phillips 1831.

LOWTHER, Lady Elizabeth (d. 1869).
Sitting 1811 : 91 × 71 : Earl of Lonsdale, Penrith.
Exhib. B.I. 1833 (17).
Appendix III (103).

LYNDHURST, Sarah (Brunsden), Lady (1795–1834).
R.A. 1828 (66) : 92 × 71 : Lord Aberdare.
Mezz. S. Cousins 1836.

LYNEDOCH, Thomas Graham, 1st Baron (1748–1843).
(1) As Licut.-Gen. Sir T. Graham.
R.A. 1813 (7) : 91 × 71 : untraced.
Engr. H. R. Cook 1813.
(2) Probably R.A. 1817 (68) : 269 × 173 : painted for the Duke of Wellington, 1817 : Apsley House, London.
Mezz. T. Hodgetts 1829.
(3) *c.* 1820 : 269 × 174 : United Services Club, London (purchased 1821).
Mezz. S. W. Reynolds 1831.

LYON, Mr.
Payment 1828 : unfinished : untraced.
Appendix III (105).

LYON, Mr., sen.
Payment 1816 : unfinished : untraced.
Appendix III (106).

LYSONS, Rev. Samuel (1730–1804).
1796 : 76 × 63 : Ex Lysons sale, Bruton, Knowles & Co., Gloucester, 21 April 1887 (282) : Lindsay Fleming, Aldwick Grange.
Repr. Plate 24.

LYSONS, Rev. Daniel (1762–1834).
c. 1800 : 76 × 63 : Ex Lysons family : C. B. Trye, Hempsted Court.
Repr. Lindsay Fleming, *Memoir and Select Letters of Samuel Lysons*, 1934.

LYSONS, Mrs. Daniel (1).
See HARDY, Sarah.

LYSONS, Mrs. Daniel (2), (Josepha Catherine Cooper).
After 1810 : 91 × 71 : formerly Earl of Southesk : destroyed by fire 1921.
Appendix III (107).

LYSONS, Samuel (1763–1819).
R.A. 1799 (137) : 76 × 63 : Ex Lysons sale,

Bruton, Knowles & Co. Gloucester, 21 April 1887 (283) : H. W. Bruton s. S. 7/7 June 1921 (169) : Lindsay Fleming, Aldwick Grange.
Mezz. S. W. Reynolds 1804. *Exhib.* B.I. 1830 (83). *Repr. The Farington Diary* ed. Grieg, 1923, Vol. I.

MACDONALD, Mrs. John (Miss Graham), later Lady.
c. 1807 : 91 × 71 : Earl of Cromer, London.

MACDONALD, Julia (d. 1859), later Lady Errington.
R.A. 1829 (97) : 91 × 71 : Viscount Errington.
Mezz. S. Cousins 1831. *Exhib.* Birmingham, *Society of Artists*, 1829 (34).
Exhib. B.I. 1833 (6).

MACKENZIE, Alexander (1755?–1820), knighted 1802.
c. 1800 : 75 × 62 : National Gallery of Canada, Ottawa.
Engr. P. Condé 1801.

MACKENZIE, Hon. Mrs. Stewart.
See HOOD, Hon. Lady.

MACKINTOSH, Sir James (1765–1832).
R.A. 1804 (157) : 93 × 62 : National Portrait Gallery, London.
Engr. J. Cochran 1833.

MCINTOSH, David.
Begun *c.* 1814 : 76 × 63 : Ex McIntosh family : E. G. Pixley s. S. 22 June 1938 (62).
Appendix III (108).

MACLEAY, Alexander, F.R.S. (1767–1848).
Probably *c.* 1825 : 76 × 63 : Linnaean Society, London.
Engr. C. Fox.

MCMAHON, Rt. Hon. Sir John, 1st Bt. (1754–1817).
R.A. 1814 (237) : 91 × 71 : Ellie, Lady McMahon, London.
Mezz. C. Turner 1814.
Replica : Ex Mrs. Marrable : Christopher Spencer by whom presented to Vancouver Art Gallery, 1933.

MAGUIRE, Mrs. and Arthur Fitzjames.
R.A. 1806 (91) as *A Fancy Group* : within a feigned circle, 165 × 165 : Duke of Abercorn, London.
Engr. W. Giller, 1846, as *The Faithful Friends.* Repr. Plate 59.

MALMESBURY, James Harris, 1st Earl of (1746–1820).
R.A. 1806 (125) : 133 × 112 : Earl of Malmesbury.
Engr. W. Ward 1807.

MANBY, Captain George (1765–1854).
c. 1800 : 127 × 102 : Ex Madame Barrot 1885.
Engr. Lith. W. J. C.

MANNERS, Lady Louisa (Tollemache) (1745–1840), later Countess of Dysart.
As Juno.
R.A. 1794 (160) : 248 × 155 : Ex S. Woodburn, by whom sold to 5th Lord Monson : Lord Monson s. C. 12 May 1888 (21) : Granville Proby : John D. Rockefeller, junr., New York.
Repr. Plate 32.
There has been misunderstanding over the identity of this sitter. Pasquin confusing the portrait with no. 168 in the same exhibition, describes it as 'a whole length of Lady Emily Hobart in the character of Juno'. Newspaper criticisms describe it variously as 'Lady Manners' and 'Lady Milner'. Farington, however, records, 3 April 1794, 'Lawrence is desirous to have the whole length of Lady Manners hung in the centre at the head of the room', and the picture was known as *Lady Manners* when it was in the Monson Collection.

MANNERS, Lady Elizabeth (*c.* 1802–1886), later Lady Elizabeth Drummond.
c. 1805 : unfinished full-length : M. A. L. Drummond of Cadland.
Finished by a later hand.
Appendix III (56).

MANNERS, Lady Robert (Mary Digges) (1737–1829).
R.A. 1826 (75) : 145 × 117 : National Gallery of Scotland, Edinburgh.
Repr. Plate 113.

MANNERS-SUTTON, Charles (1755–1828), Archbishop of Canterbury.
c. 1805–10 : 76 × 63, unfinished : Mrs. M. D. C. Bright, Cheltenham.

MARIA DE GLORIA, Donna, Queen of Portugal (1819–53).
1829 : 91 × 71 : H.M. the Queen, Windsor Castle.
Engr. R. Graves, for *The Amulet,* 1833.
Exhib. B.I. 1830 (52), 1833 (34).
Repetition : Museu Nacional de Arte Antiga, Lisbon.

MARIA THERESIA, Princess, of Austria (1816–1867), later Queen of Sicily.
R.A. 1820 (122) : 79·5 × 63 : Osterreichischen Galerie, Vienna : painted at Vienna 1818.
Repr. Plate 83.

MARKHAM, Col. David (1766–1795).
R.A. 1796 (202) : 124 × 99 : Ex E. G. Markham s. C. 8 July 1932 (15) : Leggatt, London : believed to be in America.
Appendix I (48).

MARTIN, Admiral Sir George (1764–1847).
c. 1815 : 76 × 63 : Sir William Worsley, Bt., Hovingham Hall.
Ribbon of the Bath added after 1821.
Mezz. F. C. Lewis 1836.

MARTINDALE, Mrs.
Before 1795 : untraced.   Appendix I (49).

MASTER, Mrs. Thomas (Mary Dutton) (d. 1819).
Before 1795 : 74 × 62 : Ex anon. s. C. May 19, 1911 (91) (repr. cat.) : Col. Chester-Master, Cirencester.
Appendix I (50).

MAY, Mrs. Joseph (Mary Coppendale) (1745–1824).
Probably R.A. 1812 (88) : 91 × 73 : J. M. F. May, Felixstowe.
Repr. E. K. Waterhouse in *The Burlington Magazine*, February 1952.

MAY, Mrs. Joseph (Frances Maria Stert) (1772–1861).
c. 1812 : 76 × 63 : J. M. F. May, Felixstowe.

MAYOW, Mayow Wynell (1753–1807).
Payment before 1806 : 76 × 63 : Ex W. Dacres Adams : Major David Fisher-Rowe.
Engr. W. Sharp.
Appendix II (99).

MEADE, Lady Selina (d. 1872), later Countess Clam-Martinics : painted at Vienna.
R.A. 1820 (140) : 76 × 62 : Earl of Clanwilliam, London.
Engr. C. Heath 1828. *Repr.* Plate 85.

MELBOURNE, William, 2nd Viscount.
See LAMB, Hon. William.

MELVILLE, Henry Dundas, 1st Viscount (1742–1811).
R.A. 1810 (171) : 145 × 120 : Earl of Rosebery, Dalmeny.
Mezz. C. Turner 1810.

MELVILLE, Robert Dundas, 2nd Viscount (1771–1851) .
R.A. 1826 (307) : 129 × 109 : W. L. Whitaker, Pylewell Park.
Mezz. C. Turner 1827.

MEREDITH, Sir Richard, and Lady.
Before 1797 : untraced : possibly two portraits.
Appendix I (55).

METTERNICH, Clement Wenceslaus, Prince (1773–1859).
Begun 1814 : 133 × 105 : H.M. the Queen, Windsor Castle (Waterloo Chamber).
Exhib. B.I. 1830 (3).
Replica : 140 × 111 : Prince Paul von Metternich-Winneburg (1913).
Repr. Oesterreische Kunstchaetze, III, 3/4.

METTERNICH, Princess Clementine (1804–1820).
As Hebe.
1819 : 76 × 62·5 : Prince Paul von Metternich-Winneburg (1913) : painted at Vienna.
Repr. Plate 86.

MEXBOROUGH, Anne, Countess of.
See POLLINGTON, Anne, Viscountess.

MICHEL, Mrs. John (Anne Fane) (1780–1831).
First Payment 1813 : 142 × 112 : Ex property of a lady s. C. 13 December 1904 (132) : T. J. Blakeslee : estate of E. R. Bacon, New York.
Repr. Gowan.

MILDERT, William van (1765–1836), Bishop of Durham.
1829 : 142 × 112 : The Palace, Bishops Auckland.
Mezz. T. Lupton 1831.

MILLER, William Henry, M.P. (1789–1848).
1823 : 90 × 71 : Major S. V. Christie-Miller, Clarendon Park.

MILLER, Mrs. W. II.
1823 : 90 × 71 : Major S. V. Christie-Miller, Clarendon Park.

MILNER, Diana (Sturt), Lady (d. 1805).
Before 1795 : 76 × 63 : Hon. Mrs. Marten, Crichel House.
Repr. Country Life, 23 May 1925.
Appendix I (57).
See also MANNERS, LADY.

MILTON, Mary (Dundas), Viscountess (1787–1830).
c. 1806 : 75 × 62 : Earl Fitzwilliam, Milton Park.

MINTO, Gilbert, Earl of.
See ELLIOT, Sir Gilbert.

MIRZA, ABDUL HASSAN KHAN, Persian Ambassador to England.
1810 : 90 × 70 : Ex Sir Frederick A. Gore Ouseley : Seligman, New York : William M. Chadbourne, New York.
Engr. John Lucas, 1812. *Repr.* Plate 65.

MOORE, Dr. John (1729–1802).
Before 1794 : 72 × 59 : Scottish National Portrait Gallery, Edinburgh.
Engr. G. Keating 1794.
Appendix I (58).

MOORE, Dr. John (1736–1805), Archbishop of Canterbury.
R.A. 1794 (115) : 127 × 102 : Ex Peel Heirlooms s. R. & F. 29/30 November 1917 (78) : Southampton Art Gallery.

MOORE, Captain Graham (1764–1843) later Admiral Sir Graham.
R.A. 1792 (366) : 75 × 63 : National Portrait Gallery, London.
Repr. Plate 26.

MOORE, Sir John (1761–1809).
(1) Probably *c.* 1800 : 75 × 62 : National Portrait Gallery, London.
Repetition : Depot of the Gordon Highlanders, Brig O' Don.
(2) After 1804 : 76 × 63 : Ex Lt.-Gen. Sir Robert Brownrigg, by whom commissioned : Sir Nicholas Brownrigg, Bt. Similar to (1) with addition of Star of Bath.
Mezz. C. Turner 1809. *Repr.* Beatrice, Lady Brownrigg, *Life and Letters of Sir John Moore,* 1923.

MOORE, Thomas (1779–1852).
R.A. 1830 (136) : 76 × 63 : Ex John Murray, for whom painted : Sir John Murray.
Engr. W. Finden, 1836. *Repr.* Plate 118.

MORAY, Francis Stuart, 9th Earl (1737–1813).
Sitting before 1806 : 91 × 67 : Ex possibly anon. s. C. 7 December 1951 (96) : Earl of Moray.
Appendix II (102).

MORETON, Hon. Thomas (1776–1840), later 1st Earl of Ducie, and Hon. Augustus (b. 1777).
R.A. 1790 (151) : size unrecorded : untraced.
Appendix I (30).

MORGAN, William, F.R.S., (1750–1833).
R.A. 1818 (230) : 127 × 102 : Equitable Life Insurance Company, London.
Mezz. C. Turner, 1830.

MOUNT EDGCUMBE, Sophia, Countess of.
See VALLETORT, Sophia, Lady.

MOUNT EDGCUMBE, Richard, 2nd Earl of.
See VALLETORT, Richard, Lord.

MOUNTJOY, Luke Gardiner, Viscount (1745–1795).
Before 1795 : 76 × 63 : untraced.
Engr. F. Bartolozzi.

MOUNTJOY, Charles Gardiner, Viscount (1782–1831), later 1st Earl of Blessington.
(1) R.A. 1812 (65) : size unrecorded : Ex Countess of Blessington s. Gore House, 15 May 1849 (1031).
(2) Begun *c.* 1815 : unfinished : untraced.
Appendix III (21).

MOUNTJOY, Mary (Browne), Viscountess (1786–1814).
c. 1812 : unfinished full length, cut down to 76 × 63 : Ex Knoedler, London (1921).
Appendix III (112).

MOUNTSTUART, John, Lord (1767–1794).
R.A. 1795 (86) : 230 × 146 : Marquess of Bute, Dumfries House.
Repr. Plate 33.

MUDGE, Jenny (1761–1818), later Mrs. Richard Rosdew.

Before 1800 : 76 × 63 : Ex Rosdew family : Agnew : Sir Albert James Bennett, Bt. : anon. s. Andersons Galleries, N.Y., 16 November 1933 (9).
Repr. Apollo, October 1933.

MUILMAN, William Ferdinand Mogge (b. 1778).
c. 1800 : 76 × 62 : Ex J. J. Angerstein, by whom presented to H. Muilman : Jhr. J. van de Poll : Rijksmuseum, Amsterdam.

MULGRAVE, Henry Phipps, 1st Earl of (1755–1831).
(1) *c.* 1790 : 76 × 63 : Freiherr von Cramer-Klett, by whom presented to Neue Pinakothek, Munich, 1912.
Appendix I (59).
(2) Sitting 1804 : 76 × 63 : Sir Edmund Bacon, Bt.
Replica : 75 × 62 : Sir Eric Phipps 1938.
Variant : 75 × 62 : Ex anon. s. C. 3 May 1902 (90) : Sedelmeyer, 1902.

MUNDAY, Mr.
Before 1795 : untraced.
Appendix I (60).

MUNRO, Jane (Campbell), Lady.
1826 : 236 × 145 : presented by subscribers to Government House, Madras.

MUNSTER, Ernest Friedrich, Count (1766–1839).
Sitting 1820 : 133 × 105 : H.M. the Queen, Windsor Castle (Waterloo Chamber).

MURRAY, Rt. Hon. Sir George, M.P. (1772–1846).
(1) 1812 : 76 × 63 : untraced.
Star and Ribbon of Bath added *c.* 1829.
Mezz. H. Meyer 1841.
(2) Begun 1829 : size unrecorded, probably 91 × 71, unfinished : Ex anon. s. C. 25 July 1891 (94).
Appendix III (113).
Probably the portrait *engr.* Cochran 1838.
(3) *c.* 1829 : unfinished full length : untraced.
Appendix III (114).

MURRAY, Louisa Georgiana (1822–1891), later Mrs. Boyce.
R.A. 1826 (396) as *A Child* : 136 × 108 : Ex anon. s. C. 25 July 1891 (93) : Lord Iveagh : Iveagh Bequest, Kenwood.
Engr. G. Doo, 1834. *Exhib.* Bristol, Institution for Promotion of Literature, Science and Fine Arts, 1829; B.I. 1830 (59).
Repetitions : (i) 140 × 108 : Ex Louis Huth s. C. 20 May 1905 (110) : Lord Wittenham : Lady Hermione Cameron of Lochiel s. C. 4 October 1946 (8); (ii) 90 × 68 : Ex F. R. Elkington : Sedelmeyer : Rodman Wanamaker : Mrs. Virginia Bacon : Henry Frick : Frick Collection, N.Y.

CATALOGUE

MURRAY, Emily, Lady.
See DE VISME, Miss Emily.

NAPOLEON, Francois Charles Joseph (1811–32),
Roi de Rome, 1811, Duc de Reichstadt, 1818.
1819 : 57·5 × 49 : Ex Samuel Woodburn :
Princesse de Bassano, Paris : Fogg Museum,
Cambridge, Mass. : painted at Vienna.
Exhib. B.I. 1833 (9). *Repr.* Plate 84.

NASH, John (1752–1835).
R.A. 1827 (314) : 138 × 110 : Jesus College,
Oxford.
Repr. Plate 108.

NEAVE, Sir Thomas, 2nd Bt. (1761–1848).
1798 : 76 × 63 : Sir Arundell Neave, Bt.,
Llysdulas.

NEAVE, Frances Caroline (Digby), Lady (d. 1835).
R.A. 1798 (257) : 76 × 63 : Sir Arundell
Neave, Bt., Llysdulas.

NELTHORPE, Sir John, 6th Bt. (1745/6–1799).
(1) *c.* 1790 : 76 × 63 : Col. Oliver Sutton
Nelthorpe, Scawby.
(2) *c.* 1790 : 76 × 63 : Mrs. Duncombe-
Anderson, Winchester.
Appendix I (52).

NELTHORPE, Anna Maria (Willoughby), Lady
(*c.* 1749–1829).
Before 1795 : 76 × 63 : Col. Oliver Sutton
Nelthorpe, Scawby.
Appendix I (54).

NELTHORP, Miss.
c. 1820 : 91 × 71 : Ex J. H. McFadden,
Philadelphia : destroyed by fire.

NESSELRODE, Karl Robert, Graf von (1780–1862).
1818 : 142 × 111 : H.M. the Queen, Windsor
Castle (Waterloo Chamber) : painted at Aix-
la-Chapelle.
Exhib. B.I. 1830 (15).

NEWCASTLE, Henry Pelham, 4th Duke of (1785–
1851).
1807 : 240 × 147 : Ex Earl of Lincoln s. C.
4 June 1937 (55) : Oscar Cintas, Havana.
Mezz. C. Turner 1830.

NEWCASTLE, Georgiana Elizabeth (Mundy),
Duchess of (1789–1822).
c. 1807 : 240 × 147 : Ex Earl of Lincoln s. C.
4 June 1937 (56), bt. Leggatt.

NICHOLL, Sir John (1759–1838).
c. 1806 : 142 × 112 : R. I. Nicholl, Merthyr
Mawr.
Appendix II (107).

NORFOLK, Charles Howard, 11th Duke of (1746–
1815).
R.A. 1799 (76) : 124 × 99 : Duke of Norfolk,
Arundel Castle.

NORFOLK, Charlotte Sophia, Duchess of.
See SURREY, Charlotte Sophia, Countess of.

NORMANTON, Welbore Ellis, 2nd Earl of (1778–
1868).
c. 1815–24 : 107 × 81 : Earl of Normanton,
Somerley.
Repr. The Burlington Magazine, December
1903.

NORMANTON, Diana (Herbert), Countess of
(d. 1841).
R.A. 1827 (75) : 236 × 147 : Earl of Normanton, Somerley.
Exhib. B.I. 1830 (24). *Repr.* Plate 116.

NORTH, Lady Georgiana (d. 1835).
1828 : 76 × 63, unfinished : Mrs. Stevenson
Scott, N.Y.
Appendix III (115).

NORTHUMBERLAND, Charlotte Florentia (Clive),
Duchess of (1787–1866).
c. 1828 : 133 × 113 : Duke of Northumberland,
Alnwick Castle.
Mezz. W. O. Burgess 1845. *Exhib.* Dublin 1829.

NOWELL, Mr.
Begun *c.* 1810 : unfinished : untraced.
Appendix III (117).

NOUAILLE, Peter, of Greatness, Sevenoaks (1723–
1809).
c. 1806 : 142 × 112 : formerly E. W. Rudge :
destroyed by enemy action, 1940.
Appendix II (108).

NUGENT, George Nugent Grenville, Lord (1788–
1850).
1813–20 : 238 × 147 : Major E. H. T. Boileau
(on loan Ministry of Works).
Mezz. W. Ward 1822.

NUGENT, Anne Lucy (Poulett), Lady (1790-1848).
Begun 1813 : 238 × 148, unfinished : Major
E. H. T. Boileau (on loan Ministry of Works).
Lith. Head only : R. J. Lane 1830. *Repr.*
Plate 69.

NUGENT, Mrs.
See JOHNSTONE, Mrs.

OFFLEY, Hon. Mrs. Cunliffe (Hon. Emma Crewe)
(d. 1850).
Begun 1809 : 127 × 102 : Ex Marquess of
Crewe : Henry E. Huntingdon Art Gallery, San
Marino : said to have been finished by Landseer.
Repr. Collins Baker, *Cat. British Paintings ...
Huntington Library*, 1936.
Appendix III (118).

OGILVIE, Emily Charlotte (1778–1832), later Mrs.
Charles Beauclerk.
R.A. 1796 (116) : 76 × 63 : Ex T. H. Woods
s. C. 26 May 1906 (68).

CATALOGUE

Replica : 76 × 63 : Ex Lawrence s. C. 18 June 1831 (64), bt. Wansey : E. A. Fellowes s. C. 13 July 1951 (26) as *Miss Bloxam* : Hon. Mrs. Senior, London.

OGLANDER, Maria Anne (Fitzroy), Lady (d. 1855). R.A. 1817 (190) : 239 × 145 : Ex Admiral Sir Robert Fitzroy s. C. 12 December 1896 (16) : Mrs. Clarence M. Hyde : Yerkes s. American Art Association, N.Y., 19–20 February 1912 : Alfred H. Milliken s. Anderson Galleries, N.Y., 5 January 1933 (16) (repr. cat.) : Newhouse Galleries, N.Y. 1952.

OOMS, Mrs.
See PLANTA, Mrs.

ORDE, Jane (Frere), Lady (d. 1829), and her daughter, Anna Maria.
c. 1810–12 : 138 × 109 : Ex anon. s. C. 25 April 1913 (104) : Asher Wertheimer : C. F. Fowles s. N.Y., 17 January 1922 (24).

ORIEL, John Foster, Lord (1740–1828).
Begun 1808 : unfinished : untraced.
Litho (Vignette) : M. Gauci.
Appendix III (119).

OTTLEY, Mrs. William Young (Sarah Brown) (d. 1833).
1822 : 91 × 71 : Christopher Oldfield, London.
Appendix III (120).

OUVAROFF, General Theodore (1769–1824).
1819 : 134 × 106 : H.M. the Queen, Windsor Castle (Waterloo Chamber).
Exhib. B.I. 1830 (5). *Repr.* Collins Baker, *Cat. Principal Pictures, Windsor Castle*, 1937.

OWEN, Charlotte, Lady (Philipps) (d. 1829).
Sitting 1813 : 127 × 102 : Ex Sir Hugh Owen, Bt., s. C. 8 May 1897 (81) : Sedelmeyer : Eugène Kraemer : E. M. Hodgkins s. C. 29 June 1934 (34) : Messrs. Knoedler, London (1952) : largely studio work.

OXFORD, Edward (Harley), 4th Earl of (1726–1790).
c. 1790 : 127 × 102 : Ex Lady Langdale : Lord Bateman : C. K. Hill-Wood, Barton-le-Cley.

OXFORD, Susanna (Archer), Countess of (1728–1804).
c. 1790 : 127 × 102 : Ex Lady Langdale : Lord Bateman : Sir Ian Forbes Leith, Bt. Fyvie Castle.
Repr. Plate 4.

PAGET, Hon. Berkeley Thomas (1780–1842).
R.A. 1807 (17) : 75 × 62 : Lord Hylton, Ammerdown.
Repr. Plate 62.
Appendix II (110).
Variant : 76 × 63 : Marquess of Anglesey, Plas Newydd.

PALMER, James (1740–1825).
R.A. 1821 (331) : 243 × 112 : Christ's Hospital, Horsham.

PALMERSTON, Henry Temple, 2nd Viscount (1739–1802).
Before 1795 : untraced.
Appendix I (63).

PALMERSTON, Henry Temple, 3rd Viscount (1784–1865).
c. 1820 : 55 × 44, unfinished : Countess Mountbatten of Burma, Broadlands.

PALMERSTON, Emily, Lady.
See LAMB, Lady Emily.

PAOLI, General Pasquale (1725–1807).
R.A. 1799 (234) : 76 × 63 : Ex Miss Harriet Lee : the late W. H. Lee Ewart, Mont-au-Prêtre.
Repr. Plate 37.

PARNTHER, Mr.
Date unrecorded : unfinished : untraced.
Appendix III (121).

PATERSON, Mrs. Robert.
See WELLESLEY, Marianne, Marchioness of.

PATTISON, General.
R.A. 1790 (103) : 127 × 102 : untraced.
Appendix I (64).

PATTISON, William Henry Ebenezer (1801–1832), and Jacob Howell (1803–1874).
R.A. 1817 (44) : 127 × 102 : Ex Hon. Mrs. Ronald Greville : The National Trust, Polesden Lacy : begun 1811.
Mezz. J. Bromley 1834, as *Rural Amusement*.
Repr. Plate 76.

PEEL, Sir Robert, 1st. Bt. (1750–1830).
c. 1825 : 142 × 112 : Ex Peel s. Robinson and Fisher, 29/30 November 1917 (100) : Earl Peel.
Engr. H. Robinson 1834.

PEEL, Rt. Hon. Robert (1788–1850), later 2nd Bt.
R.A. 1826 (101) : 142 × 112 : Earl Peel.
Mezz. C. Turner 1828. *Exhib.* Birmingham, *Society of Artists*, 1830 (61). *Repr.* Plate 115.

PEEL, Julia (Floyd), Lady (1795–1859).
(1) R.A. 1825 (28) : 142 × 108 : Ex Peel family : Lord Michelham : Scott and Fowles, N.Y.
(2) R.A. 1827 (134) : 91 × 71 : Ex Peel family, M. Bardac, Paris : Frick Collection, N.Y.
Engr. C. Heath, 1829, for *The Keepsake. Exhib.* B.I. 1830 (55). *Repr.* Plate 101.

PEEL, Julia Beatrice (*c.* 1822–1893), later (1) Countess of Jersey, (2) Mrs. Charles Brandling.
R.A. 1828 (77) : 142 × 112 : Ex Peel s. R. F. 6 June 1907 (179) : C. Wertheimer : Sir George Cooper, Bt., Hursley Park.
Repr. Plate 103.

PELLEW, Admiral Sir Edward (1757–1833), later Viscount Exmouth.
c. 1810 : 127 × 102 : versions of this portrait belong to Viscount Exmouth, Canonteign, and Mrs. Fleetwood Pellew, Chudleigh.
Mezz. C. Turner 1815. *Exhib.* B.I. 1833 (4).

PEMBERTON, Christopher Robert (1765–1822).
c. 1815 : 91 × 71 : Stanley M. Pemberton, Washington (Sussex).
Exhib. B.I. 1833 (8).

PEMBROKE and MONTGOMERY, Catherine (Woronzow), Countess of (1783–1856).
After 1808 : 76 × 63 : Ex Leggatt Bros. 1937 : Lord Kemsley.
Engr. G. S. Facius.

PENNICOTTE, Rev. William (1726–1811).
R.A. 1800 (213) : 76 × 63 : Ex Streatfield s. C. 20 July 1906 (93) : Metropolitan Museum, N.Y.
Mezz. S. W. Reynolds.

PERCEVAL, Rt. Hon. Spencer (1762–1812).
Probably after 1800 : 75 × 62 : Ex Sir J. W. Ellis s. C. 21 February 1913 (35) : Ehrich Galls., N.Y. : Pratt s. Am. Art Ass., N.Y. 15/16 January 1937.

PERRY, James (1756–1821).
c. 1814 : size unrecorded : Ex E. Perry 1832 : lot 81 in the Lawrence sale, 18 June 1831, included 'The late Mr. Perry by Sir Thomas Lawrence, and the copy'.

PETTIWARD, Mrs.
c. 1806 : 91 × 71 : Ex Agnew 1936.
Appendix II (114).

PHILLIPS, Henry.
Probably after 1820 : 76 × 63, unfinished : Ex probably Lawrence s. C. 18 June 1831 (97) : Mrs. Norah Hayward, Highcliffe (great-granddaughter of sitter).
Appendix III (123).

PITT, Rt. Hon. William (1759–1806).
(1) R.A. 1808 (95) : 150 × 123 : Ex J. J. Angerstein for whom painted : Marquess of Lansdowne : Earl of Rosebery.
Repr. Plate 63.
Replica : 147 × 120 : Ex J. J. Angerstein, by whom presented to the Prince Regent : H.M. the Queen, Windsor Castle.
Engr. S. W. Reynolds 1837. *Repr.* Gower.
(2) A privately printed mezzotint, possibly by C. Turner, shows a variant of (1), right hand on table, left arm akimbo. It is possible that this may be identified with the portrait : Ex Miss Wilbraham : Lord Northwick s. Thirlstane House, 26 July 1859 (371) : J. Fallows

s. C. 23 May 1868 (95). It is also possible that the Miss Wilbraham portrait is identical with (1).
(3) *c.* 1807 : 269 × 173 : Ex Royal House of Hanover : Landesmuseum, Hanover.
Apparently largely studio work. Farington notes, 31 August 1807, '[Lord Mulgrave] wished Lawrence to paint a full-length of Pitt in the robes of the Chancellor of the Exchequer'. The Hanover portrait, however, shows him in plain dress.

PITT, Mrs. William Morton- (Margaret Gambier).
c. 1806 : 49 × 43, unfinished : Messrs. Knoedler, London (1952).
Appendix II (116).

PIUS VII, Pope (1742–1823).
1819 : 264 × 146 : H.M. the Queen, Windsor Castle (Waterloo Chamber) : painted at Rome.
Mezz. S. Cousins 1828. *Exhib.* B.I. 1830 (10).
Repr. Plate 90.
Sketch : 114 × 81 : Ex Lady Blessington s. Gore House, 15 May 1849 (1006) : Mitchell : C. W. Packe : Lieut.-Col. E. C. Packe, Great Glenn House.

PLANTA, Mrs. (Charlotte Augusta Papendieck) (1783–1854), later Mrs. Ooms.
c. 1804 : 76 × 63 : Mrs. Noel Ashcroft, London.

PLATOFF, Hetman, Count (1757–1818).
R.A. 1815 (163) : 261 × 161 : H.M. the Queen, Windsor Castle (Waterloo Chamber).
Exhib. B.I. 1830 (11).

PLUMER, Sir Thomas (1753–1824).
After 1813 : 76 × 63 : presented by Lord Blanesborough to Lincolns Inn, 1925.
Engr. H. Robinson 1832.

PLUMER, William, M.P. (1737–1822).
c. 1800 : 236 × 146 : Martin L. Plumer s. C. 23 March 1923 (68), bt. Campbell.
Mezz. C. Turner 1817.

POLLINGTON, Anne (Yorke), Viscountess (d. 1870), later Countess of Mexborough, and her son.
R.A. 1821 (208) : 236 × 146 : Ex Dowager Countess of Mexborough s. C 14 December 1917 (86) (repr. cat.) : Viscount Cowdray, Cowdray.

PONSONBY, William Brabazon, 1st Lord (1744–1806).
c. 1800–1805 : 127 × 102 : E. L. P. Lascelles, Midhurst.
Repr. Sir J. Ponsonby, *The Ponsonby Family*, 1929.
Appendix II (118).

PORTARLINGTON, Alexandra, Countess of.
See VANE, Lady Alexandra.

PORTER, Dr. John (*d.* 1819), Bishop of Clogher.
Before 1819 : 76 × 63 : Clonboy, Co. Monaghan.
Mezz. C. Turner 1825.

PORTLAND, William Henry Cavendish-Bentinck, 3rd Duke of (1738–1809).
1792 : 239 × 147 : The Corporation of Bristol.
Appendix I (65).

PORTUGAL, Queen of.
See MARIA DE GLORIA, Donna.

POWEL, Col. John Hare (1786–1856).
1810 : oval 76 × 63 : Mrs. T. I. Hare Powel, Rhode Island.
Repr. Pennsylvania Museum Bulletin, May 1932.

PRATT, Samuel Jackson (1749–1814).
c. 1805 : 76 × 63 : untraced.
Engr. C. Watson 1805.

PRENDERGAST, Lady.
See DALRYMPLE, Lady.

PRICE, Sir Uvedale, Bt. (1747–1829).
R.A. 1799 (294) : 76 × 63 : Ex T. Price s. C. 16 May 1893 (55) : Museum of Fine Arts, Boston, Mass.
Appendix I (66).

PRICE, Mrs.
See HARDY, Charlotte Savery.

RAGLAN, Lady.
See SOMERSET, Lady Fitzroy.

RAIKES, Mrs. Job Mathew (Charlotte Bayley), and daughter.
Payment before 1806 : 240 × 148 : Ex Sedelmeyer : Alfred H. Mulliken s. American Art Association, N.Y., 5 January 1933 (51) : Virginia Museum of Fine Arts, Richmond, U.S.A.
Repr. Gowan.
Appendix II (122).

RAMUS, Mrs.
Before 1795 : untraced.
Appendix I (68).

RAVENSWORTH, Maria Susannah (Simpson), Lady (1773–1845).
c. 1805–10 : 76 × 63 : Hon. Mrs. Hebeler, London.

RAWDON, Francis, Lord (1754–1826), later Marquess of Hastings.
Before 1795 : 76 × 63 : Earl of Loudoun (1913) : believed to have been destroyed by fire.
Appendix I (69).

READ, Mr., of the Old Jewry.
Before 1795 : untraced.
Appendix I (70).

REDESDALE, John Freeman-Mitford, 1st Baron (1748–1830).
(1) 1807 : 127 × 102 : Ex Trustees of Mrs. Barnard s. C. 12 June 1925 (75) : Ehrich Galls. s. Am. Art Ass., N.Y., 19 April 1934 (151) (repr. cat.)
Mezz. G. Clint.
(2) *c.* 1807 : 76 × 63 : Lord Redesdale, Otterburn.

REDWOOD, Abraham (1764–1838).
1791 : 91 × 64 : Redwood library and Athenaeum, Newport, Rhode Island.

REICHSTADT, Duc de.
See NAPOLEON.

RIBBLESDALE, Thomas Lister, 1st Baron (1752–1826).
Sitting 1800 : 238 × 145 : Lady Ribblesdale s. C. 10 July 1953 (9) bt. Agnew.
Appendix II (123), Appendix III (125).

RIBBLESDALE, Rebeccah (Fielding), Lady.
Sitting 1800 : 238 × 145 : untraced.
Appendix II (124), Appendix III (126).

RIBBLESDALE, Adelaide (Lister), Lady (d. 1838), later Lady John Russell.
c. 1820 : 63 × 59, unfinished : Ex 4th Lord Ribblesdale, by whom sold *c.* 1880.

RIBBLESDALE, Thomas Lister, 2nd Baron (1790–1826).
Begun 1818 : 63 × 59, unfinished : Ex 4th Lord Ribblesdale, by whom sold *c.* 1880 : believed to be in America.
Appendix III (127).

RICHELIEU, Armand Emmanuel, Duc de (1776–1822).
1819 : 135 × 107 : H.M. the Queen, Windsor Castle (Waterloo Chamber).
Repr. Collins Baker, *Cat. Principal Pictures, Windsor Castle*, 1937.
Replica : Head only, oval 76 × 63 : Musée de Besancon.
Repr. Gower.
A portrait of the Duc de Richelieu by Lawrence was exhibited in the Paris Salon, 1824 (1053).

RICHMOND, Caroline (Paget), Duchess of (1796–1874).
R.A. 1829 (102) : 244 × 152 : Duke of Richmond and Gordon, Goodwood.

RIDDELL, Mrs. Walter (Maria Woodley).
R.A. 1806 (176) : 76 × 63 : H. J. R. Bankes, Kingston Lacy.

RIDLEY, Mrs. Mathew White (Laura Hawkins) (d. 1864), later Lady Ridley.
Sitting before 1806 : 76 × 63 : Viscount Ridley, Blagdon.
Appendix II (125).

RIPON, Frederick John, 1st Earl of.
See ROBINSON, Hon. Frederick John.

RIPON, Sarah, Countess of.
See ROBINSON, Lady Sarah.

ROBERTSON, Mrs. Francis.
Probably before 1810 : 239 × 147 : the Tate Gallery.
Apparently largely studio work; bequeathed to the National Gallery by the sitter's husband, 1838, as by Lawrence.

ROBINSON, Hon. Frederick (1746–1792).
R.A. 1793 (231) : 127 × 102 : Lady Lucas, Woodyates Manor.

ROBINSON, Hon. Frederick John (1782–1859), later Viscount Goderich, and 1st Earl of Ripon.
c. 1824 : 91 × 71 : Commander C. G. Vyner, Studley Royal.

ROBINSON, Lady Sarah (Hobart) (d. 1867), later Viscountess Goderich, and Countess of Ripon.
Payment 1824 : oval, unfinished, *c.* 76 × 63 : Commander C. G. Vyner, Studley Royal.
Appendix III (75).

ROBINSON, Emma, Lady.
See BLENCOWE, Mrs. Robert Willis.

ROBINSON, Mrs. Henry, and son.
Before 1810 : 239 × 145 : Ex Blakeslee s. 11 April 1902 (157) : C. A. Griscom s. Am. Art Ass., N.Y., 26/27 February 1914 (29) : Mrs. W. R. Coe, N.Y.
Perhaps to be identified with Appendix II (126); possibly a Lawrence design, but almost certainly largely studio work.

ROCKE, Mrs. Richard (Susannah Pattle).
Payment 1813 : 60 × 49 : unfinished : Ex Major W. L. Rocke : M. C. Brunner, Paris, 1914 : Newhouse Galleries, N.Y. (1937).
Appendix III (26).

ROLLE, John Rolle, Baron (1750–1842).
c. 1820 : *c.* 220 × 145 : Lord Clinton, Bicton.
Mezz. C. Turner 1826.

ROLLE, Louisa Barbara (Trefusis), Lady (1796–1885).
1827 : unfinished : untraced.
Appendix III (128).

ROME, Roi de.
See NAPOLEON.

ROMILLY, Sir Samuel, M.P. (1757–1818).
c. 1810 : 75 × 62 : National Portrait Gallery.
Mezz. S. W. Reynolds.

ROMILLY, Anne (Garbett), Lady (d. 1818).
Payment 1816 : unfinished : Lord Romilly, Chilton Folliat.
Appendix III (129).

ROSE, Samuel (1767–1804).
R.A. 1795 (168) : 76 × 63 : Ex Charles Burney, s. C. 31 March 1922 (32) : anon. s. C. 26 June 1925 (41) : A. L. Nicholson, London (1926).
Mezz. C. Turner 1810.

ROUSE, Benjamin (1742–1814).
1813 : 91 × 71 : Commercial Union Assurance Co. Ltd., London.
Mezz. C. Turner 1815.
Appendix III (130).

ROYSTON, Philip, Viscount (1784–1808).
c. 1806 : unfinished full-length : Earl of Hardwicke, Rockley Manor.
Appendix II (127), Appendix III (131).

ST. ALBANS, Louisa (Manners), Duchess of (1777–1816).
Sitting before 1806, oval 71 × 62 : Ex Lady Charlotte Bruce, Lady Laura Tollemache, Marchioness of Ailesbury, s. R. & F. 27 June 1901 (147).
Appendix II (134).

ST. GERMANS, William, 2nd Earl of (1767–1845).
c. 1800 : 75 × 61 : Earl of St. Germans, Port Eliot.

ST. JOHN of BLETSOE, Louisa (Rouse-Boughton), Lady (d. 1860), later Lady Vaughan.
Begun *c.* 1809 : 239 × 147, unfinished : Ex Lord St. John of Bletsoe s. C. 4 July 1913 (133) : Knoedler : Morton F. Plant, U.S.A. (1917) : finished by a later hand.
Repr. W. Roberts in *The Connoisseur*, February 1915.
Appendix III (138).

ST. LEGER, Hon. Mrs. Richard (Anne Blakeney) (d. 1809).
c. 1806 : 76 × 63 : Viscount Doneraile, Doneraile Court.
Appendix II (136).

SABLOUKOFF, Madame (Juliana Angerstein) (d. 1846).
(1) Before 1806 : 76 × 63 : Col. Michael Barne, Sotterley Park.
(2) Before 1806 : 75 × 62 : Ex George Harland-Peck s. C. 25 June 1920 (92) : Viscount Bearsted s. C. Lord Baldwin's Fund for Refugees, 25 May 1939 (247) : Schneider Galleries, N.Y.

SALE, Florentia (Wynch), Lady (1790?–1855).
After 1820 : 76 × 63 : untraced.

SALISBURY, Frances Mary (Gascoyne), Marchioness of (1802–1839).
R.A. 1829 (193) : 244 × 142 : Marquess of Salisbury, Hatfield.
Engr. W. Ensom, for *Literary Souvenir*, 1831.

CATALOGUE

SALTOUN, Alexander George Fraser, 16th Lord (1785–1853).
Payment 1809 : 238 × 147 : United Service Club, London.
Appendix III (132).

SANDWICH, Louisa, Countess of Sandwich.
See HINCHINBROOKE, Louisa Lady.

SANDYS, Marcus, Lord.
See HILL, Lord Marcus.

SANSOM, Philip (d. 1815).
c. 1810–15 : 127 × 101 : National Gallery.
Repr. National Gallery, *Illustrations, British School*, 1936.

SCHWARZENBERG, Charles Philip, Prince of (1771–1820).
1818 : 314 × 239 : H.M. the Queen, Windsor Castle (Waterloo Chamber) : painted in Vienna.
Exhib. B.I. 1830 (89).

SCOTT, Sir Walter (1771–1832).
R.A. 1827 (146) : 155 × 133 : H.M. the Queen, Windsor Castle.
Engr. J. H. Robinson, 1833. *Exhib.* B.I. 1833 (26). *Repr.* Plate 109.

SCOTT-WARING, Mrs.
See ESTEN, Mrs.

SEAFORD, Charles Rose Ellis, 1st Baron (1771–1845).
c. 1829 : 127 × 102 : Marquess of Bristol, Ickworth.

SEAFORTH, Francis Humberston Mackenzie, 1st Baron (1754–1815).
R.A. 1798 (51) : 236 × 145 : Ex Louisa, Lady Ashburton : Private Collection, France.
Exhib. B.I. 1830 (71). *Repr.* Plate 34.

SEAHAM, George Henry, Viscount (1821–1884), later 5th Marquess of Londonderry.
R.A. 1824 (392) : 76 × 63 : Marquess of Londonderry, London.
Exhib. B.I. 1830 (69). *Repr.* H. M. Hyde, *Londonderry House and its Pictures*, 1937.

SHAFTESBURY, Earl of.
See COOPER, Hon. C. A.

SHAW-BROOKE, Rev. J. K.
c. 1800 : 75 × 62 : Ex Mrs. Barnard, Cave Castle. s. C. 12 June 1925 (76), bt. Leggatt.

SHEEPSHANKS, Mr.
Before 1795 : untraced.
Appendix I (71).

SHEEPSHANKS, Miss.
Payment 1828 : unfinished : untraced.
Appendix III (134).

SHEPHERD, Sir Samuel (1760–1840).
R.A. 1796 (183) : 127 × 102 : untraced.
Mezz. J. R. Jackson 1846.

SHERIDAN, Richard.
See ATHERLEY, Arthur.

SHERIDAN, Richard Brinsley (1751–1816).
c. 1790–95 : 127 × 102 : Ex Lord Young s. C. 29 February 1908 (40) : Sir Edward Stracey (1913) : Messrs. Leggatt, London (1926).
The identification with Sheridan is doubtful, but the portrait is certainly by Lawrence.

SIDDONS, Mrs. William (Sarah Kemble) (1755–1831).
(1) Possibly R.A. 1797 (166) : 76 × 63 : Ex Miss Harriet Lee : the late W. H. Lee Ewart, Mont-au-Prêtre.
Engr. C. Turner 1826 for Boaden's *Siddons*. *Repr.* Plate 43.
Pasquin's description of the R.A. 1797 portrait as depicting youth and 'flexibility' of feature ... 'to denote a lady who is so proverbially stern in her countenance' applies to this rather than any other known portrait of Mrs. Siddons by Lawrence. Whitley, however, quotes reviewers who describe the portrait as a full-length. It is unlikely that (1) has been cut down from a full-length.
(2) *c.* 1797 : 76 × 63 : Ex Mrs. Coombe (Cecilia Siddons), by whom bequeathed to the National Gallery 1868.
Possibly the '2nd portrait of Mrs. Siddons' mentioned by Farington, 2 January 1797.
(3) *c.* 1797 : 76 × 63 : by family descent to Alice, Lady Butler, London : variant of (2).
Repr. Cat. *Lawrence Exhibition*, Brighton, 1951.
(4) R.A. 1804 (193) : 254 × 147 : presented by Mrs. C. FitzHugh to the National Gallery, 1843.
(5) A three-quarter length 'half finished' portrait was claimed by Mr. Fitzhugh from the executors of Lawrence (Appendix III). This may be identical with the unfinished portrait (similar to (1)) : Ex Mrs. McIlwaine : formerly Ehrich Galls., N.Y.

SIDDONS, Miss Sarah (1775–1803).
A number of portraits claim to represent this sitter. Two only seem likely to have any connection with her and in neither case is the identity proved.
(1) *c.* 1800 : 75 × 62 : Ex G. Morant s. 16 April 1847 (243) : Hogarth s. C. 13 June 1851 (44) : E. Bicknell s. C. 25 April 1863 (37) : Lord Hertford : Wallace Collection.
Repr. Plate 45.
(2) *c.* 1800 : 143 × 112 : Ex Capt. R. S. Fraser-Mackenzie s. C. 1 July 1927 (126) : A. L. Nicholson s. Am. Art Ass., N.Y., 18 May 1933 (24).

SIDDONS, Miss Maria (1779–98).
Among the portraits called *Maria Siddons* one only is certainly by Lawrence and may represent her.
Before 1798 : 76 × 63 : Duke of Bedford, Woburn Abbey.
Mezz. G. Clint. *Exhib*. B.I. 1830 (73). *Repr*. Plate 44.
Cecilia Siddons in a letter to Archibald Keightley, 2 June 1830, wrote, with particular reference to this portrait, 'Neither of Mrs. Siddons' daughters ever sat to Lawrence for an oil picture, and also . . . none of the family recollect ever to have heard that he painted one from memory' (letter in National Portrait Gallery archives).

SIMEON, Rebeccah (Cornwall), Lady (d. 1830).
Before 1800 : 76 × 63 : Ex Simeon family : Agnew : Horace Trumbauer : French and Co., N.Y.

SINCLAIR, Rt. Hon. Sir John, 1st Bt. (1754–1835).
c. 1790 : 72 × 58 : Viscount Sinclair, Caithness.
Engr. W. Skelton 1790.

SINGLETON, Hon. Mrs. James.
See UPTON, Hon. Caroline.

SKIPWITH, Selina (Shirley), Lady (1752–1832).
1829 : 85 × 71 : Major Evelyn Shirley, Loch Fea.
Exhib. Birmingham, Society for Promoting the Fine Arts, 1829 (62).

SMITH, Robert Percy, ('Bobus') (1770–1845).
c. 1800–1805 : 75 × 62 : Ex W. G. Trower s. C. 8 July 1927 (54) : A. Rofe, London.

SMITH, Sir Sidney (1765–1840).
Before 1800 : 76 × 63 : Ex J. Anderson, Coxlodge Hall : Rev. Hector de Courcelles 1906.

SMITH, Mrs. John (probably Elizabeth Leigh, 3rd wife of John Smith of Midhurst, d. 1851).
After 1811 : 76 × 63 : Lt.-Col. O. W. D. Smith, Earl's Croome.

SNEYD, Miss Emma, of Byrkley Lodge.
Before 1806 : 76 × 63 : Hon. Mrs. Fitzroy-Newdegate, Arbury.
Appendix II (130).

SOANE, Sir John, R.A. (1753–1837).
R.A. 1829 (338) : 142 × 112 : The Sir John Soane Museum, London.
Mezz. C. Turner 1830. *Exhib*. B.I. 1830 (85).

SOMERSET, Lady Fitzroy (Emily Harriet Wellesley) (d. 1881), later Lady Raglan.
c. 1820 : 76 × 62·5 : Ex Raglan family until *c*. 1912 : The Hermitage, Leningrad.
Repr. Les Chefs D'Œuvres . . . de L'Hermitage, Munich, 1923.

SOMERVILLE, Maria Lady.
See CONYNGHAM, Lady Maria.

SONDES, Lewis Thomas, 2nd Earl (1754–1806).
Before 1795 : untraced.
Appendix I (72).

SONDES, Mary (Milles), Countess (d. 1818).
Before 1795 : untraced.
Appendix I (73).

SOPHIA, H.R.H. Princess (1777–1848).
R.A. 1825 (57) : 140 × 112 : H.M. The Queen, Windsor Castle.
Repr. Plate 104.

SOTHEBY, William (1757–1833).
Sitting 1807 : 53 × 41, unfinished : Lt.-Col. H. G. Sotheby, Ecton Hall.
Appendix II (131).

SOTHERON, Admiral Frank, M.P. (1765?–1839).
1809 : 127 × 102 : T. E. Sotheron-Estcourt, Estcourt.
Mezz. C. Turner 1839.

SOTHERON, Lucy, later Mrs. T. G. Bucknell-Estcourt.
c. 1820 : 128 × 102 : T. E. Sotheron-Estcourt, Estcourt.

SOUTHEY, Robert (1774–1843).
R.A. 1829 (172) : 142 × 112 : Ex Peel s. R. & F. 2 February 1910 (190); Sir Abe Bailey : South African National Gallery, Cape Town.
Engr. (Vignette), J. T. Wedgewood 1829. *Repr*. Plate 110.

SPENCER, George John, 2nd Earl (1758–1834).
Before 1795 : untraced.   Appendix I (74).

SPENCER, Hon. Edward (1779–1823).
c. 1810 : 75 × 62 : Ex W. G. Trower s. C. 8 July 1927 (55) : Litchfield s. P-B, N.Y., 11 October 1951 (89).

STAFFORD, George Granville Leveson-Gower, 2nd Marquess of (1758–1833), later 1st Duke of Sutherland.
c. 1824 : 76 × 63 : Duke of Sutherland, Dunrobin.
Mezz. S. W. Reynolds, junior., and W. Walker, 1839. *Repr. Les Arts*, January 1913.

STAFFORD, Elizabeth, Marchioness of (1765–1839), suo jure Countess of Sutherland; later Duchess of Sutherland.
R.A. 1816 (48) : 76 × 63 : Duke of Sutherland, Dunrobin.
Engr. H. Meyer. *Repr. Les Arts*, January 1913.

STANLEY, Lord Edward Smith, M.P. (1775–1851), later 13th Earl of Derby.
(1) *c*. 1790 : 53 × 46 : Earl of Derby, Knowsley Hall.
(2) 1793 : 76 × 63 : The Provost's Lodge, Eton College.

STANLEY, Hon. Charlotte Margaret (Hornby), Lady (1776–1817).
c. 1790–95 : 76 × 63 : Earl of Derby, Knowsley Hall.

STEWART, Lord Charles (1778–1854), later 3rd Marquess of Londonderry.
(1) As *Major-General the Hon. C. Stewart.*
R.A. 1811 (88) : half-length : untraced.
(2) As *Lieut.-General Sir Charles Stewart.*
R.A. 1813 (159) : 127 × 102 : Ex Prince Troubetskoi : Marquess of Londonderry, London.
Engr. H. Meyer 1814. *Repr.* Plate 72.
Replica : 127 × 102 : Marquess Camden, Bayham Abbey.
Exhib. B.I. 1830 (25), 1833 (25).
(3) As *Lord Charles Stewart.*
1818 : 76 × 63 : Marquess of Londonderry, London : painted at Vienna.

STEWART, Lady Caroline Anne (Pratt) (1794–1827).
c. 1825 : 76 × 63 : Marquess Camden, Bayham Abbey.

STEWART, Lady Catherine Anne (Bligh) (d. 1812), with her son, Frederick, later 4th Marquess of Londonderry.
c. 1807 : 234 × 137 : Marquess of Londonderry, Wynyard Park.

STEWART, Hon. Frederick (1805–1872), later 4th Marquess of Londonderry.
R.A. 1818 (139) : 89 × 57 : Marquess of Londonderry, London.
Repr. H. M. Hyde, *Londonderry House and its Pictures*, 1937.
Repetition : 71 × 57 : Ex Marquess of Londonderry, anon. s. C. 25 April 1903 (84) : C. J. Wertheimer, 1911.
Repr. Gowan.

STONESTREET, George (1744/5–1802).
R.A. 1802 (421) : 127 × 102 : Phoenix Assurance Company, London.

STORER, Hon. Mrs. Thomas (Elizabeth Proby), (1752–1808).
Sitting before 1806 : 251 × 161 : Ex Major A. M. Storer, s. S. 24 March 1920 (146).
Appendix II (137), Appendix III (139).

STOWELL, William Scott, Baron, F.R.S. (1745–1836).
R.A. 1824 (38) : 140 × 109 : Ex Peel s. R. & F. 29/30 November 1917 (96).

STRANGE, Sir Thomas (1756–1841).
1820 : 239 × 147 : presented by subscribers to Government House, Madras.
Mezz. C. Turner 1820.

STRATTON, Mrs. George Frederick (Anne d'Ewes).
(1) *c.* 1811 : 76 × 64 : Ex Knoedler, N.Y. : Nathan Allan, 1910.
(2) R.A. 1811 (69) : 239 × 149 : John & Mable Ringling Museum, Sarasota.
Mezz. C. Turner. *Repr.* Plate 70.

STUART, General James (1741–1815).
R.A. 1801 (62) : 127 × 102 : Possibly the portrait (Ex Major D'Arcy Irvine of Fermanagh) now in the City Art Museum, St. Louis.
Mezz. G. Clint 1802. It is known that this portrait was copied by Lane.

SUFFIELD, Caroline, Lady.
See HARBORD, Caroline, Lady.

SUFFOLK, John Howard, 15th Earl of, and 8th Earl of Berkshire (1739–1820).
R.A. 1818 (148) : 127 × 102 : Margaret Countess of Suffolk and Berkshire, Redlynch Park.

SURREY, Charlotte Sophia (Leveson-Gower), Countess of (1788–1870), later Duchess of Norfolk.
c. 1815–20 : 76 × 63 : Duke of Norfolk, Arundel Castle.
Engr. J. Thomson 1825.

SUTHERLAND, Elizabeth, Duchess of.
See STAFFORD, Elizabeth, Marchioness of.

SUTHERLAND, Harriet, Duchess of.
See GOWER, Harriet, Countess.

SUTTON, Sir Richard, 2nd Bt. (1799–1855), Mary Elizabeth (Burton), Lady (d. 1842), and child.
Payment 1824 : 274 × 193 : C. R. Sutton, Newbury.
Repr. The Field, 4 August 1927.
Appendix III (140).

SYDNEY, Caroline (Clements), Viscountess (d. 1805).
Payment 1854 : 58 × 48, unfinished : Ex Earl Sydney : Mortimer L. Schiff s. C. 24 June 1938 (73).
Appendix II (138), Appendix III (141).

SYKES, Sir Mark Masterman, 3rd Bt. (1771–1823), Henrietta (Masterman), Lady (d. 1813), and Tatton (1772–1863), later 4th Bt.
Payment before 1806 : 236 × 181 : Sir Richard Sykes, Bt., Sledmere.
Repr. Plate 68.
Appendix II (139).

SYKES, Elizabeth (Egerton), Lady (d. 1846), later Mrs. Stratford Dugdale.
After 1814 : 127 × 102 : Sir Richard Sykes, Bt., Sledmere.

SYKES, Beatrice Hester Decima (d. 1843), later Mrs. J. R. Foulis.

Before 1806 : 76 × 63 : Sir Richard Sykes, Bt., Sledmere.
Appendix II (142), Appendix III (69).

TALBOT, Lord Charles (1777–1849), later 2nd Earl Talbot, and Lord John (1779–1825).
c. 1792 : 224 × 219 : Earl of Shrewsbury, Ingestre.
Repr. Plate 14.
Appendix I (75).

TASKER, Captain John, of the East India Company.
R.A. 1790 (268) : untraced.

TAUNTON, Henry, 1st Lord.
See LABOUCHERE, Henry.

TAYLOR, Thomas (1758–1835).
R.A. 1812 (228) : 125 × 100 : Ex Major W. B. Mynors : National Gallery of Canada, Ottawa.

TAYLOR, Lieut.-General Sir Herbert (1775–1839).
Payment 1807 : 71 × 63 : Ex anon. s. C. 20 May 1927 (46), bt. Knoedler : Henry Reinhardt, N.Y. (1927).
Probably Appendix II (143).

TAYLOR, John, F.R.S. (1779–1863).
Payment 1826 : 127 × 102 : destroyed by fire 1870.
Mezz. C. Turner 1831.
Appendix III (143).

TCHERNITSCHEFF, Alexander Ivanovitch, Prince (1779–1957).
1818–19 : 129 × 103 : H.M. the Queen, Windsor Castle (Waterloo Chamber) : painted at Vienna.
Exhib. B.I. 1830 (4).

TEMPLETOWN, Mary (Montagu), Lady (d. 1824), with her son, Henry (1799–1863), later 2nd Viscount Templetown.
R.A. 1802 (5) : 215 × 150 : Ex Alfred de Rothschild : Countess of Carnarvon : Andrew Mellon : National Gallery of Art, Washington.
Repr. Plate 48.

THAYER, Miss, later Baroness Adolphe Thiebault.
R.A. 1813 (63) : 76 × 63 : Lady Craigmyle, Fairnilee House.
Exhib. B.I. 1830 (46).

THELLUSON, Mrs. Charles (Sabine Robarts) (1775–1814), with her son Charles (1797–1856).
R.A. 1804 (17) : 244 × 142 : Mrs. Grant-Dalton, Brodsworth Hall.

THIEBAULT, Baroness Adolphe.
See THAYER, Miss.

THOMAS, Mrs. James.
See WOODGATE, Maria.

THOMOND, Murrough O'Brian, 1st Marquess of.
See INCHIQUIN, Murrough O'Brian, 5th Earl of.

THOMOND, Mary, Marchioness of.
See INCHIQUIN, Mary, Countess of.

THOMPSON, Mr.
R.A. 1798 (253) : untraced.

THOMSON, Mrs. John (Charlotte Jacob) (d. 1824), and son, Charles Edward (1799–1841), later Lord Sydenham.
Begun before 1806 : 224 × 147 : Ex George Poulett Scrope, M.P. : E. T. Stotesbury s. P-B, N.Y. 18 November 1944 (15) : Oscar Cintas, Havana.
Appendix II (145).

THURLOW, Edward Thurlow, 1st Baron (1731–1806).
R.A. 1803 (21) : 126 × 101 : H.M. the Queen, Windsor Castle.
Repr. Plate 51.

TORRENS, Major-General Sir Henry, K.C.B. (1779–1828).
R.A. 1816 (161) : *c.* 244 × 142 : Ex J. A. Berners of Woolverstone Park : Barbara, Lady Nash, by whom presented to the Corporation of Londonderry, 1950.
Mezz. C. Turner 1817.

TOWRY, Mrs. George Philips.
c. 1805 : 76 × 63 : Ex Lord Ellenborough s. C. 28 May 1895 (143) : Ralph Cross Johnson : Smithsonian Institute, Washington.
Appendix II (146).

TRACY, John Tracy, 7th Viscount, D.D. (1722–1793).
c. 1790 : 75 × 60 : All Souls College, Oxford.
Engr. C. Knight.

TRENCH, Mrs. R.
Begun 1815 : full-length as St. Cecilia, unfinished : untraced.
Appendix III (145).

TRIMLESTOWN, Alicia (Eustace), Lady (1773–1860), later Lady Evan Lloyd.
Begun *c.* 1800 : 224 × 147 : Ex Mrs. Evan Lloyd : James Orrock s. C. 4 June 1904 (104). Viscount Leverhulme s. Anderson Gallery, N.Y. 17–19 February 1926 (104) (repr. cat.).
Apparently largely studio work.
Appendix II (147).

TRITTON, George (1761–1831).
c. 1800–10 : 144 × 112 : Mrs. Leslie Tritton, Lyons Hall.
Mezz. W. Say.

TROWER, Mrs. John (Jane James).
c. 1810–15 : 75 × 62 : Ex W. G. Trower s. C. 8 July 1927 (53) : Gov. Alvan T. Fuller, Boston, Mass.

CATALOGUE

TWISS, General William (1745–1827).
c. 1805 : 76 × 63 : W. H. Ferrand, Bilton Dene.

TWISS, Mrs. Horace (Frances Kemble) (1759–1822).
R.A. 1800 (526) : 75 × 62 : Ex Horace W. Twiss s. C. 20 June 1930 (104) (repr. cat.).

UPTON, Hon. Sophia (d. 1853).
R.A. 1801 (173) : 76 × 63 : Ex Viscount Templetown s. K.F.R. 26 May 1911 (71) : E. T. Stotesbury s. P–B, N.Y., 18 Nov., 1944. (7).
Repr. Plate 47.

UPTON, Hon. Caroline (d. 1862), later Mrs. James Singleton.
R.A. 1801 (190) : 76 × 63 : Ex Viscount Templetown s. K.F.R. 26 May 1911 (72).
E. T. Stotesbury s. P-B, N.Y., 18 November 1944 (8).
Repr. Plate 46.

VALLETORT, Richard, Lord (1764–1839) later 2nd Earl of Mount Edgcumbe.
1790 : 76 × 63 : painted for Lord Valletort's tutor Dr. Drake : Charles Peel, London : Howard Young, N.Y., 1929.
Appendix I (76).

VALLETORT, Sophia (Hobart), Lady (1768–1806), later Countess of Mount Edgcumbe.
c. 1790 : 76 × 63 : Ex Henry Reinhardt Galleries, N.Y., 1925.
Appendix III (111).

VANE, Lady Alexandra (1824–1874), later Countess of Portarlington.
1827–8 : 76 × 63 : Marquess of Londonderry, London.
Repr. H. M. Hyde, *Londonderry House and its Pictures*, 1937.

VAUGHAN, Rt. Hon. Sir Charles Richard (1774–1849).
After 1820 : 104 × 80 : All Souls College, Oxford.
Mezz. S. Cousins.
Repetition : c. 91 × 71 : Lt.-Col. the Hon. J. Fremantle, Wistow Hall.

VAUGHAN, Louisa, Lady.
See ST. JOHN OF BLETSOE, Louisa, Lady.

VENOUR, Mrs. Walter Askell (Helen Davidson) (1796–1843).
1817–22 : 76 × 63 : Mrs. Venour, Nairn.

VERNON, Henry, 3rd Lord (1747–1829).
Probably after 1820 : 236 × 145 : Lord Vernon, Sudbury Hall.

VIVIAN, John, of Claverdon (1756–1828).
c. 1800–05 : 91 × 71 : by family descent to Mrs. Vivian-Neal, Poundisford Park.

VIVIAN, Mrs. John (Marianne Edwards) (c. 1775–1826).
c. 1800–05 : 91 × 71 : by family descent to Mrs. Vivian-Neal, Poundisford Park.

VYNER, Theodosia Maria (Ashburnham), Lady (1765–1822).
R.A. 1791 (75) : 127 × 102 : Major E. R. F. Compton, Newby Hall.
Repr. Plate 5.
Appendix I (77).

WALLSCOURT, Elizabeth (Locke), Lady (1805-1877).
R.A. 1826 (65) : 91 × 71 : Ex Lord Wallscourt : C. Wertheimer : H. J. Joel, St. Albans.
Engr. W. Ensom, for *The Bijou*, 1829. *Repr.* Plate 97.

WARD, John, of Stramshall (1756–1829).
Before 1800 : 127 × 102 : Ex anon. s. C. 4 July 1919 (51) : Leger, London (1930).
Mezz. J. Grozer.
Possibly Appendix II (148).

WATERFORD, Henry de la Poer, 2nd Marquess (1772–1826).
Probably c. 1814 : 254 × 152 : Marquess of Waterford, Curraghmore.

WATERFORD, Susannah (Carpenter), Marchioness of (d. 1827).
Sitting 1814 : unfinished : untraced.
Appendix III (149).

WATSON, Juliana, Lady.
See COPLEY, Miss Juliana.

WATT, James (1736–1819).
R.A. 1813 (222) : 140 × 112 : Miss Boulton, Tew Manor.
Mezz. C. Turner 1815. *Exhib.* Liverpool Academy 1813 (31).

WEDGEWOOD, Mrs. John (Louisa Jane Allen) (1771–1836).
Sitting before 1806 : 76 × 63 : Mrs. Clement Allen, Woodchester 1915.
Repr. H. Litchfield and E. Darwin, *A Century of Family Letters 1792–1896*, 1915.
Appendix II (149).

WELLESLEY, Richard, Marquess (1760–1842).
R.A. 1813 (208) : 127 × 102 : H.M. the Queen, Windsor Castle.
Mezz. C. Turner 1815.
Repetitions : (1) The Castle, Dublin; (2) Eton College.

WELLESLEY, Marianne (Caton), Marchioness (formerly Mrs. Robert Paterson) (d. 1853).
(1) When Mrs. Paterson.
c. 1817 : 76 × 63 : Duke of Wellington, Strathfield Saye House.

CATALOGUE

(2) As Marchioness Wellesley.

Lawrence is said to have painted a portrait of this sitter after her marriage to Marquess Wellesley in 1825, which is, or was, in a private collection in Baltimore, U.S.A. This may have been the unfinished portrait delivered to the Marchioness in 1831.

Appendix III (150).

WELLESLEY, Hon. Richard (1787–1831).
c. 1805–08 : 91 × 71 : The Provost's Lodge, Eton College.

WELLINGTON, Arthur Wellesley, Duke of (1769–1852).
(1) Sitting 1814 : 254 × 152 : Marquess of Londonderry, Wynyard Park.
(2) *c.* 1814 : 91 × 71 : Apsley House, London.
Repr. Plate 71.
(3) R.A. 1815 (109) : 315 × 225 : H.M. the Queen, Windsor Castle (Waterloo Chamber).
Engr. W. Bromley, 1818. *Exhib.* B.I. 1830 (9).
Repr. Collins Baker, *Cat. Principal Pictures, Windsor Castle*, 1937.
(4) R.A. 1818 (165) : 396 × 243 : Earl Bathurst, Cirencester.
Repr. Gower.
Replica : 140 × 96 : painted for J. J. Angerstein : W. Angerstein s. C. 4 July 1896 (116).
Engr. W. Bromley.
(5) R.A. 1822 (134) : 75 × 62 : Ex General Arbuthnot s. C. 29 June 1878 (88) : Earl of Rosebery s. 5 May 1939 (81) : Private Collection.
Mezz. S. Cousins 1828. *Repr.* Plate 93.
(6) R.A. 1825 (71) : 251 × 96 : Ex Peel s. R. & F. 25 November 1909 (190) : Wellington College, Berks.
Exhib. B.I. 1830 (53).
(7) Probably after 1820 : 63 × 51, unfinished : Ex Sir Robert Peel for whom painted : Duke of Buccleuch, Bowhill.
(8) *c.* 1825–30 : 97 × 76, unfinished : Earl of Jersey.
Repr. Armstrong.
(9) After 1820 : 239 × 157 : said to have been purchased at one of the Lawrence sales : R. Napier of Shandon : Lord Kinnaird : Viscount Esher : finished by Simpson.

WEST, Benjamin, P.R.A. (1738–1820).
(1) R.A. 1811 (113) : 152 × 121 : Ex West family : Castle Smith s. Paris, 21 June 1913 : anon. s. C. 27 April 1928 (130).
Engr. H. Meyer 1813.
(2) *c.* 1811 : 76 × 62, unfinished : Ex Lawrence sale, 19 June 1830 (419), bt. Hutchinson :

J. H. Anderson : H. N. Pym s. C. 22 November 1912 (70) : Amherst College, Amherst, Mass.
Repr. Plate 73.
(3) R.A. 1821 (193) : 269 × 177 : Wadsworth Atheneum, Hartford, Conn.
Replica : Painted for George IV, and presented by William IV to the National Gallery, 1836 : Tate Gallery.
Engr. C. Rolls 1842. *Exhib.* B.I. 1830 (78), 1833 (II). *Repr.* Gower.

WEST, Harriet (1804–1879), later Mrs. William Woodgate.
1825 : 76 × 63 : Ex anon. s. C. 23 February 1907 (82) : J. H. Mcfadden : Philadelphia Museum of Art.
Repr. Gowan.

WESTMINSTER, Elizabeth, Marchioness of.
See LEVESON–GOWER, Lady Elizabeth.

WESTMORLAND, John, 10th Earl of (1759–1841).
(1) 1807 : 90 × 68 : N. C. B. Clive Ponsonby-Fane, Brympton D'Evercy.
Mezz. S. W. Reynolds and S. Cousins.
Appendix II (151).
(2) *c.* 1806 : 236 × 145 : N. C. B. Clive-Ponsonby-Fane, Brympton D'Evercy.
Appendix II (152).

WHEATLEY, Louisa (Hawkins), Lady.
Before 1810 : 91 × 71 : Ex Col. Moreton Wheatley : E. C. Converse Estate, N.Y., 1927.
Repr. Armstrong.

WHITBREAD, Lady Elizabeth (Grey) (1765–1846).
R.A. 1793 (7) : 76 × 63 : Ex Barnet Lewis s. C. 28 February 1930 (100) : Earl Grey, Howick.
Repr. Gowan.

WHITWORTH, Charles, Earl (1752–1825).
(1) Sitting 1807 : 122 × 96 : Ex Countess Delawarr 1868 : presumably identical with C. Sackville-Bale s. C. 14 May 1881 (232) : Louvre.
Mezz. C. Turner 1814. *Repr.* Gower.
Appendix II (153).
(2) A 'whole-length portrait of Lord Whitworth in his Robes' was included in the Lawrence sale, C. 18 June 1831 (99).

WIGRAM, Sir Robert, Bt., M.P. (1743–1830).
c. 1815 : 127 × 102 : Miss FitzWygram.
Engr. J. H. Watt 1833.

WIGRAM, Eleanor (Watts), Lady (d. 1841).
c. 1815 : 220 × 145 : Miss FitzWygram.
Mezz. C. Turner 1817. *Exhib.* B.I. 1830 (68).

WILBERFORCE, William (1759–1833).
Begun 1828 : 96 × 109, unfinished : Ex Sir

CATALOGUE

R. H. Inglis, Bt., by whom commissioned National Portrait Gallery, London.
Engr. anon. 1838. *Repr.* Plate 119.
Appendix III (151).

WILDMAN, Colonel.
Untraced.
Appendix III (152).

WILLIAM IV, King.
See CLARENCE, Duke of.

WILLIAMS, Thomas, of Temple House (d. 1802).
Possibly R.A. 1789 (51) : 127 × 102 : at Temple House until *c.* 1930 : Mlle Colas and Countess Vanutelli, Paris, *c.* 1935.

WILLIAMS, Lewis (1766–1808).
c. 1793 : 76 × 63 : Ex Valentine Rowe s. C. 26 June 1914 (73) : Knoedler, N.Y. : Vandyck Galleries, Washington, 1924.
Appendix I (79).

WILLIAMS, Raby (1768–1808).
c. 1793 : 76 × 63 : Ex Valentine Rowe s. C. 26 June 1914 (72) : Knoedler, N.Y. : Mrs. J. Van Nostrand Dorr, N.Y.
Repr. Plate 27.
Appendix I (80).

WILLIAMS, Mrs. John, of Gwersylt (Elizabeth Currie).
(1) Possibly R.A. 1804 (25) : 76 × 63 : Ex Major W. G. Townsend Currie s. C. 3 June 1932 (64).
(2) *As St. Cecilia.*
Begun 1804 : *c.* 236 × 145 : Ex Col. Moreton Wheatley, Gwersylt Park (1913) : finished by Hilton.
Lith. R. J. Lane.
Appendix III (153).
(3) *c.* 1804 : 127 × 102 : Ex anon. s. C. 27 July 1945 (126) : Lord Mackintosh of Halifax.
Similar to (2) and conceivably (2) cut down.

WILLIAMS, Mrs. John (Harriet Davenport), later Lady (d. 1861).
Probably after 1820 : 91 × 69, unfinished : Dr. Sheffield Neave, Ingatestone.

WILLIS, John, M.D.
Begun 1829 : 236 × 145 : The Lawn Hospital, Lincoln. Largely studio work.
Appendix III (154).

WILLOUGHBY D'ERESBY, Clemintina Sarah.
See DRUMMOND, Lady Clementina Sarah.

WILSON, Thomas.
Payment 1803 : finished 1815 : untraced.
Appendix III (156).

WILSON PATTEN, Mrs., (Anna Maria Bold), (d. 1846).
Begun 1829 : unfinished : Earl of Scarbrough, London.
Appendix III (122).

WILTON, Mary, (Stanley), Countess of (1801–1858).
c. 1825 : 145 × 114 : Ex Earl of Wilton : Roussel s. Gal. G. Petit, Paris, 27 May, 1932,
Mezz. G. H. Philips, 1838. *Repr.* Armstrong.

WINDHAM, Rt. Hon. William, M.P., (1750–1810).
R.A. 1803 (105) : 127 × 102 : University College, Oxford.
Mezz. S. W. Reynolds.
Appendix II (156).

WINDSOR, Baroness.
See CLIVE, Lady Harriet.

WOLFF, Mrs. Jens (Miss Hutchinson) (d. 1829).
(1) Probably before 1810 : 58 × 47 : Ex Archibald Keightley : Miss Mary Keightley : Major O. G. S. Croft, Hephill.
(2) R.A. 1815 (28) : 127 × 101 : Ex W. W. Kimball : Art Institute, Chicago.
Mezz. S. Cousins 1831. *Repr.* Plate 77.

WOLFF, George.
Probably *c.* 1810 : 76 × 63 : Guy C. Rogers, Stanage Park.

WOOD, Lady Caroline (Stewart) (d. 1865).
Finished 1829 : 76 × 63 : Mrs. Hore-Ruthven, Bracondale Woods.

WOOD, son of Mr., and dog.
Unfinished : untraced.
Appendix III (157).

WOODBURN, Samuel (1786–1853).
c. 1820 : 109 × 83 : Fitzwilliam Museum, Cambridge.
Exhib. B.I. 1830 (84). *Repr.* Gowan.

WOODFORD, Sir Ralph, Bt. (1784–1828).
R.A. 1830 (79) : 236 × 145 : Legislative Council Chamber, Red House, Port of Spain.
Mezz. C. Turner 1829.

WOODGATE, Maria (1803–1833), later Mrs. James Thomas.
c. 1823 : 75 × 62 : Ex James Woodgate Arbuthnot : Knoedler, N.Y. : Mrs. B. F. Jones, junior., s. P-B., N.Y., 4/5 December. 1941.

WOODGATE, Mrs. William.
See WEST, Harriet.

WOOLL, Rev. John (1767–1833).
c. 1810 : 91 × 71 : untraced.
Mezz. C. Turner 1813.

WORCESTER, Georgiana, (Fitzroy), Marchioness of (d. 1821).
c. 1817 : 76 × 63 : Duke of Wellington, Strathfield Saye House.
Repetition : 76 × 63 : Duke of Beaufort, Badminton.
Exhib. B.I. 1833 (20).

CATALOGUE

WORONZOW, Count Simon.
Sitting before 1806 : 76 × 63 : the Hermitage, Leningrad.
Repr. Les Chefs d'Œuvres . . . de l'Ermitage, Munich, 1923.
Replicas : 76 × 63 : (1) Earl of Pembroke and Montgomery, Wilton; (2) Sir Michael Duff, Bt. Appendix II (158).

WORONZOW, Prince Michael (1782–1856).
R.A. 1822 (35) : 127 × 102 : the Woronzow family, The Crimea, 1943.
Engr. S. W. Reynolds 1823.

WRIGHT, Mrs. Ichabod.
See Day, Miss Harriet.

WYATT, Edward (1757–1833).
c. 1800 : 127 × 102 : untraced.
Engr. J. Godby 1810.

WYATVILLE, Sir Jeffrey (1766–1840).
(1) 1828 : 142 × 112 : H.M. the Queen, Windsor Castle.
Engr. H. Robinson. *Exhib.* B.I. 1830 (79).
(2) 1828 : 80 × 65, unfinished : Ex anon. s. Gal. Charp. Paris, 27 April 1951 (29).
Appendix III (159).

WYNN, Sir Watkin Williams-, 5th Bt. (1772–1840).
Before 1795 : 76 × 63 : Dowager Lady Williams-Wynn, Belan.
Appendix I (81).

WYNN, two children of Sir Watkin Williams-, Bt., Payment 1826 : unfinished : not now in family possession; possibly destroyed in the fire at Wynnstay, 1858.
Exhib. B.I. 1830 (88*).
Appendix III (161).

YARDE-BULLER, Mrs. John (Elizabeth Wilson-Patten) (d. 1857).
1827 : 76 × 63, unfinished : Lord Churston, Churston Court.
Appendix III (32).

YORK, Frederick, Duke of (1763–1827).
(1) R.A. 1814 (64) : half-length : possibly Ex A. L. Nicholson, London : R. Pyne s. Am. Art Ass., N. Y., 12/13 January 1940 (235).
(2) R.A. 1816 (61) : 279 × 180 : H.M. the Queen, Windsor Castle (Waterloo Chamber).
Mezz. Three-quarters only : C. Turner 1830.
Exhib. B.I. 1830 (88).
Repetition, Commissioned 1825 : 279 × 180 : Merchant Taylors Company, London.
(3) R.A. 1822 (73) : 76 × 63 : untraced.
Engr. G. Doo 1824.

YORK, Archbishop of.
See HARCOURT, Edward Venables Vernon.

YORK, Whitwell (d. 1817).
Probably after 1810 : 76 × 63 : Christopher York, Marston Manor.
Mezz. C. Turner 1814.

YORKE, John (1776–1857).
Begun 1826 : 76 × 63 : Major J. E. E. Yorke, Halton Place : finished by Simpson.
Appendix III (162).

YORKE, Mrs. John (Mary Wright) (d. 1883).
1821 : 76 × 63 : Major J. E. E. Yorke, Halton Place.

YOUNG, Thomas, M.D. (1773–1829).
Before 1820 : 91 × 71 : Q. E. Gurney, Bawdeswell Hall.
Mezz. C. Turner 1820.

SUBJECT PICTURES

CHRIST BEARING HIS CROSS
1786 : *c.* 245 × 145 : untraced.

HOMER RECITING HIS POEMS
R.A. 1791 (180) : 85 × 114 : Ex Richard Payne Knight for whom painted : Major W. M. P. Kincaid-Lennox, Downton Castle.
Repr. Plate 19.

PROSPERO RAISING THE STORM
R.A. 1793 (191) : 335 × 223 : Lawrence painted out the picture and used the canvas for *J. P. Kemble as Rolla*.

GIPSY GIRL
1794 : 89 × 58 : Royal Academy of Arts (Diploma Picture).
Mezz : S. W. Reynolds 1840.

SATAN SUMMONING HIS LEGIONS
R.A. 1797 (170) : 432 × 271 : Ex Duke of Norfolk after whose death (1815) it returned to Lawrence's possession : Lawrence sale C. 18 June 1831 (151) : Samuel Woodburn : Royal Academy of Arts.
Exhib. Bristol, Institution for Promotion of Literature, Science and the Fine Arts, 1826; B.I. 1830 (82). *Repr.* Plate 35.

LANDSCAPE : SOURCE OF THE MANIFOLD
Before 1800 : 44 × 67 : Col. H. M. Grant, London.
Engr. T. Lupton, 1834. *Repr.* Plate 21.

WOODY LANDSCAPE
Before 1800 : 44 × 67 : Col. H. M. Grant, London.
Engr. T. Lupton, 1834. *Repr.* Plate 20.

CATALOGUE

UNIDENTIFIED PORTRAITS

A LADY
  c. 1790–95 : 75 × 62 : Wallace Collection.

A LADY
  c. 1805 : 76 × 63, unfinished : City Art Gallery, Bristol.

A LADY
  c. 1820 : circular, 38 diameter : Ex Sir Charles Tennant : Lord Glenconner, Glen.

A GIRL
  *c.*1800 : oval 48 × 41 : Ex H. A. J. Munro : Novar Collection : Misses Davies : National Museum of Wales, Cardiff.
  Exhib. B.I. 1833 (23).

A GENTLEMAN
  Before 1800 : 76 × 63 : Ex S. Fox, Harrogate : G. N. Black, by whom bequeathed to Boston Museum of Fine Arts, 1924.
  At one time called *C. J. Fox.*

A GENTLEMAN
  c. 1800–1805 : 76 × 63 : Louvre.

APPENDIX I

Compiled from two lists published by D. E. Williams in *The Life and Correspondence of Sir Thomas Lawrence, Kt.*, 1831. The original lists were, presumably, among family papers and are not known to survive today. They cannot be accepted as wholly reliable as some portraits appear to be entered twice with different prices, in which case only one entry is quoted below.

	Gns.		*Gns.*
(1) Son of Lord Abercorn	15	(31) Miss Farren	100
(2) Daughter of Lord Abercorn	15	(32) Mr. Gataker	15
(3) Mrs. Adair	10	(33) Duchess of Gordon	15
(4) Princess Amelia	15	(34) Lord Cecil Hamilton	15
(5) Mr. Anderson	25	(35) Sir G. Heathcote	30
(6) Mrs. Annesley	120	(36) Mr. Hornsby (*sic.*)	40
(7) Lady Apsley	20	(37) Miss Hornsby (*sic.*)	40
(8) Mrs. Armistead	50	(38) Mr. Hunter	30
(9) Mr. Atherley	50	(39) Mrs. Johnson	15
(10) Lord Barrington	30	(40) Mr. Kelly	15
(11) Lady Basset's Daughters	50	(41) Lord Lauderdale	25
(12) Sir G. Beaumont	15	(42) Mr. Law	25
(13) Lord Belmour (*sic.*)	50	(43) Lady Louisa Lennox	15
(14) Lady C. Bentinck	25	(44) Mr. Locke	25
(15) Mr. Beresford	55	(45) Young Mr. Locke	25
(16) Hon. Mrs. Berkeley	20	(46) Mr. Long	20
(17) Captain Berkeley	20	(47) Lady J. Long	25
(18) Mrs. Berwick	25	(48) Captain Markham	25
(19) Duchess of Buccleuch	30	(49) Mrs. Martindale	25
(20) Mr. Capper	20	(50) Mrs. Masters	30
(21) Lord G. Cavendish	70	(51) Lord Melbourne's Children	40
(22) Mr. Cholmondely	25	(52) Sir J. Melthorpe (*sic.*)	25
(23) Lord Cremorne	40	(53) His Niece	25
(24) Lady Cremorne	40	(54) Lady Melthorpe (*sic.*)	25
(25) Miss Day	25	(55) Sir R. and Lady Meredith	30
(26) Mr. Darnsey (*sic.*)	15	(56) Mr. Miller	25
(27) Lord Douglas	25	(57) Lady Milner	25
(28) Mr. Douglas	15	(58) Dr. Moore	25
(29) Major Doyle	25	(59) Lord Mulgrave	15
(30) Lord Ducie's Sons	80	(60) Mr. Munday	25

APPENDIX I

	Gns.		*Gns.*
(61) Lady Newdicote (*sic.*)	25	(72) Lord Sondes	30
(62) Mrs. Nugent	15	(73) Lady Sondes	30
(63) Lord Palmerston	30	(74) Lord Spencer	30
(64) General Pattison	40	(75) Lord G. Talbot's sons	60
(65) Duke of Portland	100	(76) Lord Valletort	25
(66) Mr. Price	25	(77) Lady Theo. Viner	30
(67) Queen	80	(78) Mr. Watts	15
(68) Mrs. Ramus	30	(79) Mr. Williams	15
(69) Lord Rawdon	25	(80) Mr. Raby Williams	15
(70) Mr. Read (Old Jewry)	20	(81) Sir W. W. Wynne	30
(71) Mr. Sheepshanks	25		

APPENDIX II

Compiled from: (i) 'List of Pictures painted & painting by Thomas Lawrence Esq. Copied from a Statement which Mr. Lawrence corrected the 14th February 1806.' The list was drawn up at the request of Thomas Coutts at a time when Lawrence was near bankruptcy, and is now in the possession of Coutts Bank Ltd. (ii) Various additions made to the same list on 24th February 1806 and 18th February 1807.

For whom painted	Price £ s. d.	Received on account £ s. d.	For whom painted	Price £ s. d.	Received on account £ s. d.
1. Abercorn, the Marquess of	126 0 0	—	27. Bute, The Marchioness of	126 0 0	—
2. Aberdeen, Lord (¾)	—	21 0 0	28. Campbell, Lady Charlotte	126 0 0	63 0 0
3. Aberdeen, Lady	147 0 0	73 10 0	29. Canterbury, The Dean of	63 0 0	31 10 0
4. Abrams, Miss	42 0 0	21 0 0	30. Carbery, Lord	147 0 0	—
5. Ancram, Lady	42 0 0	21 0 0	31. Cassillis, Lady	—	84 0 0
6. Annesley, Mrs.	147 0 0	73 10 0	32. Castlereagh, Lord	36 15 0	18 7 0
7. Baillie, Dr.	36 15 0	18 7 0	33. Cholmondeley, Mr. Geo.	31 10 0	—
8. Baker, Mr.	73 10 0	36 15 0	34. Chudd, Mrs.	36 15 0	18 7 0
9. Baker, Mrs. (¾)	—	21 0 0	35. Clements, Miss	73 10 0	36 15 0
10. Barnard, Mrs.	52 10 0	26 5 0	36. Clive, Lord	36 15 0	18 7 0
11. Barnard, Mrs. T.	63 0 0	15 15 0	37. Craven, Lord	126 0 0	63 0 0
12. Barton, Mrs., and child	157 10 0	89 5 0	38. Dalrymple, Miss	36 15 0	18 7 6
13. Barwells, The Mr.	147 0 0	73 10 0	39. Darnley, Lord	147 0 0	—
14. Bath, Lady, and 3 children	230 10 0	100 0 0	40. Dashwood, Miss	36 15 0	18 7 0
15. Beckford, Miss	36 15 0	18 7 0	41. Dean, General (¾)	—	21 0 0
16. Blackshaw, Mrs.	47 5 0	23 12 6	42. Derby, Lady, and her child	63 0 0	—
17. Blantyre, Lady	63 0 0	31 10 0	43. Dottin, Mr.	350 0 0	175 0 0
18. Bligh, Lady Catherine	147 0 0	73 10 0	44. Douglass, Mr.	31 10 0	15 15 0
19. Boughton, Miss	126 0 0	63 0 0	45. Drummond, Miss	105 0 0	52 10 0
20. Bradshaw, Mrs. Cavendish	126 0 0	63 0 0	46. Dupre, Mr.	73 10 0	23 12 6
21. Brandling, Mrs. C.	47 5 0	23 12 6	47. Dupre, Mrs.	147 0 0	73 10 0
22. Brandling, Mr. William	47 5 0	23 12 6	48. Ellenborough, Lord	84 0 0	42 0 0
23. Brown, Mrs.	73 10 0	36 15 0	49. Elliott, Mr.	31 10 0	—
24. Brown, Mr.	73 10 0	36 15 0	50. Elliott, Miss	15 15 0	—
25. Burdett, Sir Francis	126 0 0	63 0 0	51. Esten, Mrs.	147 0 0	73 10 0
26. Bute, The Marquess of	126 0 0	—			

For whom painted	Price £ s. d.	Received on account £ s. d.
52. Exeter, Lady, and her child	126 0 0	—
53. Fane, Lady G.	73 10 0	36 15 0
54. Fane, Lady Maria	168 0 0	84 0 0
55. Fitzgerald, Miss	36 15 0	18 7 6
56. Fitzpatrick, General	31 10 0	15 15 0
57. Fludyers, Lady, and children	210 0 0	105 0 0
58. Forster, Lady Eliza	126 0 0	63 0 0
59. Fox, Mr. (for Mr. Bouverie)	31 10 0	—
60. Francis, Mr.	31 10 0	—
61. Godfrey, Mrs.	31 10 0	—
62. Gordon, Lady William	47 5 0	23 12 6
63. Grant, Mrs.	31 10 0	15 15 0
64. Grantham, Lord (¾)	42 0 0	—
65. Grey, The Hon. Chas.	63 0 0	31 10 0
66. Grey, Mrs. Chas., and children	210 0 0	105 0 0
67. Grigg, Mrs.	100 0 0	50 0 0
68. Halket, Mrs.	126 0 0	63 0 0
69. Hamilton, Dr.	31 10 0	—
70. Hamlet, Mrs. Thomas	50 0 0	—
71. Hamond, Sir Andrew	31 10 0	15 15 0
72. Hampden, Lord	84 0 0	—
73. Hare, Mr.	31 10 0	15 15 0
74. Harvey, Mr.	147 0 0	73 10 0
75. Hawkins, Mrs., and child	50 0 0	50 0 0
76. Heathcote, Sir Gilbert	147 0 0	73 10 0
77. Henry, Mr.	47 5 0	20 0 0
78. Hereford, Lord	42 0 0	20 0 0
79. Hervey, Lady Louisa, and children	168 0 0	84 0 0
80. Hinchinbrooke, Lady	147 0 0	73 10 0
81. Hope, Mr. H. P.	168 0 0	84 0 0
82. Howard, Mr.	36 15 0	—
83. Impey, Mrs.	31 10 0	15 15 0
84. Inglis, Miss	73 10 0	36 15 0
85. Innes, Miss	63 0 0	31 10 0
86. Jones, Mrs.	47 5 0	20 0 0
87. Lamb, Mr. G.	36 15 0	—
88. Lamb, Mr. Willm.	36 15 0	18 7 0
89. Lascelles, Mrs.	31 10 0	—
90. Lee, Miss	36 15 0	18 7 6
91. Legh, Mr.	84 0 0	21 0 0
92. Leigh, Mrs.	47 5 0	23 12 6
93. Leitrim, Lady, and child	105 0 0	52 10 0
94. Leveson, Lord G.	147 0 0	73 10 0
95. Lorn, Marquis of	126 0 0	—
96. Lowther, Miss	147 0 0	73 10 0
97. Malmesbury, Lord	73 10 0	36 15 0
98. Manners, Lady G.	73 10 0	36 15 0
99. Mayow, Mr.	42 0 0	21 0 0
100. Melville, Lady	47 5 0	—
101. Monk, Miss	36 15 0	—
102. Moray, Lord (Kit-cat)	—	26 5 0
103. Morris, Mr.	36 15 0	15 15 0
104. Murray, Mrs. (¾)	42 0 0	21 0 0
105. Nesbitt, Mr. T.	126 0 0	63 0 0
106. Nesbitt, Mrs.	147 0 0	73 10 0
107. Nicholl, Sir John	42 0 0	—
108. Noaille, Mr.	73 10 0	36 15 0
109. Ooms|s|, Mrs.	—	21 0 0
110. Paget, Mr. B.	36 15 0	18 7 0
111. Paget, Mr. Charles	42 0 0	—
112. Paget, Mrs. C.	36 15 0	—
113. Parnther, Mr.	31 10 0	15 15 0
114. Pettiward, Mrs.	47 5 0	23 12 6
115. Pitt, Mr. Morton	31 10 0	15 15 0
116. Pitt, Mrs. Morton	36 15 0	18 7 6
117. Pitt, Miss Morton	31 10 0	15 15 0
118. Ponsonby, Mr.	63 0 0	31 10 0
119. Ponsonby, Mrs.	63 0 0	31 10 0
120. Portland, The Duke of	63 0 0	—
121. Powis, Earl (late Lord Clive)	63 0 0	31 10 0
122. Raikes, Miss	168 0 0	84 0 0
123. Ribblesdale, Lord	126 0 0	63 0 0
124. Ribblesdale, Lady	126 0 0	63 0 0
125. Ridley, Mrs.	47 5 0	23 12 6
126. Robinson, Mrs.	73 10 0	36 15 0
127. Royston, Lord (whole-length)	—	84 0 0
128. Siddons, Mrs.	31 10 0	—
129. Simpson, Lady (for Miss Simpson)	126 0 0	63 0 0
130. Sneyd, Miss (Kit-cat)	26 5 0	—
131. Sotheby, Mr.	31 10 0	15 15 0
132. Spencer, Mr. William	31 10 0	—
133. St. Albans, The Duke of	126 0 0	—
134. St. Albans, The Duchess of	31 10 0	—
135. Stewart, Col.	31 10 0	—
136. St. Leger, Mrs.	47 5 0	23 12 6

APPENDIX II

For whom painted	Price £ s. d.	Received on account £ s. d.	For whom painted	Price £ s. d.	Received on account £ s. d.
137. Storer, Mrs.	126 0 0	63 0 0	149. Wedgewood, Mrs.	31 10 0	15 15 0
138. Sydney, Lady	47 5 0	23 12 6	150. Wentworth, Lord	—	21 0 0
139. Sykes, Sir M. M.	315 0 0	157 10 0	151. Westmorland, Lord	42 0 0	—
140. Sykes, Lady	63 0 0	52 10 0	152. Westmorland, Lord (whole-length)	168 0 0	—
141. Sykes, Lady	105 0 0	52 10 0	153. Whitworth, Lord	84 0 0	—
142. Sykes, Miss	84 0 0	42 0 0	154. Williams, Mr.	36 15 0	18 7 6
143. Taylor, Colonel	52 0 0	26 5 0	155. Williams, Mrs.	147 0 0	73 10 0
144. Thomas, Mrs.	47 5 0	—	156. Windham, Mr.	31 10 0	15 15 0
145. Thomson, Mrs., and child	183 15 0	—	157. Wolff, Mr.	47 5 0	—
146. Towry, Mrs. (¾)	—	21 0 0	158. Woronzow, Count	220 10 0	—
147. Trimblestone, Lady	126 0 0	63 0 0	159. Woronzow, Countess (copy)	36 15 0	—
148. Ward, Mr.	47 5 0	23 12 6			

APPENDIX III

The following list is taken from *The Claims of Works of Art, Books etc. under the Estate of the late Sir Thomas Lawrence* drawn up by Archibald Keightley, Lawrence's executor.   The manuscript is now in the Victoria and Albert Museum (MSS. English, 86 H 19).

Claimant	Sitter	Date of sitting or payment	Condition
1. Lord Aberdeen	The late Lady Aberdeen		Unfinished
2. Lord Ailesbury	Lady Ailesbury	1809 and 1812	About ⅔ finished
3. Mr. Allnutt	'Mr. Allnutt's Daughter'	Begun 1826	Head nearly finished
4. Lady Suffield	Lady Ancram		Head only
5. Mr. Annesley	Mrs. Annesley and two children	'Begun 30 yrs. since'	About ⅔ finished
6. Duke of Argyll	Himself	1817	¾ finished
7. Duke of Argyll	Duchess of Argyll		Head only
8. Lady Arundel	The late Lord and Lady Arundel	Begun about 1812	About ½ finished
9. Col. H. Baillie	Miss Baillie	1827	About ⅔ finished
10. Mr. Baker	Mrs. Baker	About 1812	About ½ finished
11. Mr. Balfour	His Father		
12. Princess Elizabeth Bariatinsky	The late Princess Bariatinsky		Head not finished
13. Sir Thos. Baring	The Heads of Sir Thos. B's Son and Nephew		About ½ finished
14. Mr. Henry Baring	Portrait of himself cut out of a larger picture		
15. Mrs. Barton	Miss Barton	1829	Not ½ finished; only sketched in chalk
16. Mrs. Munday	Mr. Edwd. and Mr. C. Barwell in one group as boys		
17. Marquess of Bath	Marchioness of Bath and children	1804	About ⅔ finished
18. Sir J. Le Beauvoir	Himself		¾ finished
19. Sir John Beckett	Himself	1826	Head finished
20. Lord Belfast	Lady Belfast	Payment 1825	Nearly finished
21. Lord Beresford	Himself	1818	Head painted, figure sketched

APPENDIX III

Claimant	Sitter	Date of sitting or payment	Condition
22. Lord Blessington's executors	Late Earl of Blessington	1815 or 16	$\frac{4}{5}$ finished
23. Lord Bloomfield	Himself	1827 or 8	Sketch on Canvas
24. Mrs. Zornlin	Mr. Bolland		Finished
25. Mrs. Thomson Bonar	Herself	Payment 1813	$\frac{1}{2}$ finished
26. Mrs. Bond	Herself when Mrs. Rocke	Payment 1813	Small half length little more than $\frac{1}{2}$ finished
27. Mr. Boulton	Himself	Payment 1828	Head only
28. Hon. A. C. Bradshaw	Himself		Full length, head finished, figure drawn.
29. Hon. A. C. Bradshaw	Mrs. Bradshaw		$\frac{1}{2}$ length, head finished
30. Mr. R. W. Brandling	Mrs. Brandling	1804	Head only
31. Duke of Buckingham	Duchess of Buckingham		
32. Mr. Yarde Buller	Mrs. Yarde Buller	Payment 1828	Head nearly finished
33. Duchess of St. Albans	Sir F. Burdett	1793	Head finished, figure sketched
34. Earl of Egremont	Lady C. Burrell	Payment 1829	Head only
35. Mr. C. Calvert	Mrs. Calvert	1825 or 6	Whole length, head nearly finished
36. Lord Carbery	Himself		$\frac{3}{4}$ finished
37. Lord Carlisle	Himself		Head not finished
38. Earl of Cassillis	Lady Cassillis	c. 1810	Whole length, not half finished
39. Lord Charlemont	Lady Emily Caulfield		
40. Lord Cawdor	Lady Cawdor	Payment 1827	Head only
41. Lord Cawdor	Himself	Payment 1829	Head only
42. Sir Richard Sutton	Mr. F. Chaplin	1825	
43. Lord Clive	Lady Lucy Clive	Payment 1826	About half finished
44. Hon. Robert Clive	Lady Harriet Clive	1823 or 4	Nearly finished
45. Hon. Robert Clive	Himself	1808	Head only
46. Mrs. Cludde	Late Mrs. Cludde	Payment 1806	$\frac{3}{4}$ finished
47. Sir E. Codrington	Himself	1826	Finished
48. Sir E. Codrington	Lieut. Codrington	1829	Head not finished
49. Lord Combermere	Himself	Payment 1815	Head finished
50. Lord Sefton	Lord Craven	Payment 1802	Head finished, figure drawn
51. Mrs. Williams	Mrs. Davenport	1827	Finished
52. Mr. Dingwall	Mrs. Dingwall	Payment 1825	Head not finished
53. Mr. Dottin	Mr. and Mrs. Dottin and Mrs. Dottin's sister	Begun 1798	Heads painted
54. Miss Douglas	Herself		Hair painted and outline of face
55. Mr. Droop	Mrs. Droop	Payment 1823	Head finished
56. Duke of Rutland	Lady Elizabeth Drummond	Payment 1805	
57. Lord Duncannon	Lady Duncannon	1805	Head finished, figure partly drawn
58. Mr. Egerton	Mrs. Egerton	c. 1805	Not $\frac{1}{2}$ finished
59. Mr. Scott (for the Native Education Society, Bombay)	Hon. Mr. Elphinstone	1829	Head nearly half finished
60. Mr. Esdaile	Himself	1829	Not $\frac{1}{2}$ finished

Claimant	Sitter	Date of sitting or payment	Condition
61. Lord Essex	Himself	1829	Finished
62. Lord Exeter	Marchioness of Exeter	1829	½ finished
63. Lord Exeter	Children of 10th Marquess of Exeter	Payment 1800	About ⅔ finished
64. Mr. John Fairlie	Mrs. John Fairlie	1827	Full length, head finished
65. Lord Farnham	Himself	Payment 1827	½ finished
66. Mr. Vernon	Mr. Fawcett	1828	Head nearly finished
67. Mr. Fitzgerald	Mrs. Fitzgerald	Payment 1825	Nearly ½ finished
68. Lord Milton	Earl Fitzwilliam	Payment 1827	About ¾ finished
69. Mr. Egerton	Mrs. Foulis		Not ½ finished
70. Mrs. Lane Fox	Herself	1829	Nearly ½ finished
71. Lord Stafford	Mrs. Fraser of Lovat	Payment 1823	
72. Mr. Fullarton	His niece and daughter	1825	About ⅔ finished
73. Earl of Galloway	Lady Galloway		Head only
74. Lady Gifford	Late Lord Gifford	1825	Head begun
75. Lord Goderich	Lady Goderich	Payment 1824	About ½ finished
76. Lady Wm. Gordon	Herself	Begun c. 1807	Finished
77. Duke of Gordon	Himself	c. 1825	Nearly finished
78. Rev. Walter Trower	Mrs. Goring	Payment 1809	About ½ finished
79. Duke of Grafton	Himself	Payment 1816	About ⅔ finished
80. Mrs. Prendergast	Mrs. Grant	1801	Head only
81. Lady Guilford	Herself	Payment 1829	Not ½ finished
82. Mr. Fitzhugh	Dr. Hamilton (two portraits)		Finished
83. Sir H. Hardinge	His two sons	1829	Not ½ finished
84. Lady Louisa Harvey	Herself and two children	c. 1800	3 heads not finished
85. Lady Felton Harvey	Late Sir Felton Harvey		
86. Mr. Prince Hoare	Himself	c. 1826–7	Head finished
87. Mr. Hope	His Brother in a Turkish dress	1805	About ½ finished
88. Mr. Peel	Mr. Huskisson		½ finished
89. Lord Ingestre	Lady S. Ingestre		Not ½ finished
90. Lord Jersey	Himself	1815	Head finished
91. Mr. G. F. Jones	Sir Rd. Jones	1827	Head nearly finished
92. Lord Blessington's Executors	Mr. Kemble as Cato		
93. Sir W. Knighton	Lady Knighton	1827	Head nearly finished
94. Mr. W. Ponsonby	Lady Caroline Lamb	1809	Head finished
95. Marquess of Lansdowne	Himself	Payment 1827	⅔ finished
96. Mr. G. L. Leigh	Mrs. Leigh	c. 1805	Not more than ½ finished
97. Prince Lieven	Himself		Finished
98. Bishop of Lincoln	Himself	Payment 1828	Not ½ finished
99. Mr. W. Lockhart	Mrs. Lockhart	Payment 1826	Head finished
100. Mr. Lomax	Mrs. Lomax	Payment 1827	About ½ finished
101. Lord Londonderry	Emily, Lady Londonderry		Head finished
102. Lord Lonsdale	Lady Lonsdale	Payment 1817	About ⅔ finished
103. Lord Lonsdale	Lady Elizabeth Lowther	Payment 1811	
104. Marquess of Lothian	Himself	Payment 1824	

APPENDIX III

Claimant	Sitter	Date of sitting or payment	Condition
105. Mr. Lyon	Himself	Payment 1828	About ¾ finished
106. Mr. Lyon	Mr. Lyon, senr.	Payment 1818	Head not finished
107. Rev. Mr. Lysons	Mrs. Lysons		
108. Mr. McIntosh	Himself	1813 or 1814	About ½ finished
109. Mr. Mayow	Himself		
110. Mr. Mayow	Mrs. Mayow	Payment 1828	
111. Lady Suffield	Lady Mount Edgecumbe		
112. Lord Blessington's Executors	Late Countess of Mount-joy		Head finished, figure sketched
113. Sir G. Murray	Himself		Nearly ½ finished
114. Major Belches	Sir G. Murray (full length for the County of Perth)	1829	2 sittings only
115. Lady Guilford	Lady Georgiana North	Payment 1828	Full length, head finished
116. Lady Guilford	Lady Susan and Lady Georgiana North	1810	Heads finished
117. Mr. Nowell	Himself	c. 1810	Full length, nearly finished
118. Mr. Cunliffe Offley	Mrs. Cunliffe Offley	Begun 1809	¾ finished
119. Lord Ferrard	Late Lord Oriel	Payment 1808	⅔ finished
120. Mr. Ottley	Mrs. Ottley		
121. Mr. Parnther	Himself		Not ½ finished
122. Mrs. Wilson Patten	Herself	Payment 1828	Head about ½ finished
123. Mr. H. Phillips	Himself		Head not finished
124. Mrs. Prendergast	Herself	1801	Nearly finished
125. Lord Ribblesdale	Late Lord Ribblesdale	1800	Finished
126. Lord Ribblesdale	Late Lady Ribblesdale	1800	Finished
127. Lord Ribblesdale	Himself	1818	Head finished, figure drawn
128. Lord Rolle	Lady Rolle	Payment 1827	Head nearly finished
129. Mr. Wishaw	Lady Romilly	Payment 1816	Head finished
130. Hand in Hand Fire Office	Mr. Rouse		
131. Lord Hardwicke	Late Lord Royston	c. 1804–7	
132. Lady Saltoun	Lord Saltoun	Payment 1809	About ¾ finished
133. Countess of Sandwich	Herself	Payment 1804	
134. Miss Sheepshanks	Herself	Payment 1828	Head only
135. Mr. Fitzhugh	Mrs. Siddons		Half finished ¾ length
136. Mr. John Smith	His two daughters-in-law when children	1817	Not more than half finished
137. Mr. W. Sotheby	Himself, two portraits		Unfinished
138. Baron Vaughan	Lady St. John		Whole length, head only
139. Mrs. Storer	Late Hon. Mrs. Storer		Not ½ finished
140. Sir Richard Sutton	Himself, Lady Sutton and child	Payment 1824	About ½ finished
141. Hon. J. R. Townshend	Lady Sydney	Begun 1805	Head finished
142. Mr. Egerton	Lady Sykes		Finished
143. Mr. J. Taylor	Himself	Payment 1826	Finished
144. Mrs. Gwatkin	Late Marchioness of Thomond		½ finished

Claimant	Sitter	Date of sitting or payment	Condition
145. Mr. R. Trench	Mrs. R. Trench as St. Cecilia	Begun 1815	Whole length, head only
146. Lady Trimleston	Herself	1800	
147. Mr. G. Vernon	Lady Elizabeth Vernon	Payment 1823	$\frac{2}{3}$ finished
148. Mrs. Scott Waring	Herself when Mrs. Esten	Payment 1800	
149. Marquess of Waterford	Marchioness of Waterford	Payment 1814	About $\frac{1}{6}$ finished
150. Marchioness Wellesley	Herself		$\frac{3}{4}$ finished
151. Sir R. H. Inglis	Mr. Wilberforce	Payment 1828	Not $\frac{1}{2}$ finished
152. Mrs. Wildman	Col. Wildman		Head not finished
153. Mr. John Williams	Mrs. Williams	Payment 1804	Full length, about $\frac{1}{3}$ finished
154. Dr. Willis	Himself	1829	Head half finished
155. Lord Willoughby	Lady Willoughby when Miss Drummond	c. 1805	
156. Mr. Thos. Wilson	Himself	Payment 1803	Finished in 1815
157. Mr. Wood	Mr. Wood's son and dog		About $\frac{1}{2}$ finished
158. Marquess of Worcester	Marchioness of Worcester	c. 1820	$\frac{3}{4}$ finished
159. Sir Jeffry Wyattville	Himself	1827–8	Head finished
160. Mr. Wyndham	Himself	1827	About $\frac{1}{2}$ finished
161. Sir Watkin W. Wynn	His two children	Payment 1826	Heads finished
162. Mr. Yorke	Himself	1828	Head finished

INDEX OF COLLECTIONS

GREAT BRITAIN AND IRELAND

HER MAJESTY THE QUEEN

WINDSOR CASTLE
Alexander, Emperor of Russia
Princess Amelia
Duc d'Angoulême
Earl Bathurst
Prince von Blucher
Duke of Cambridge
George Canning (studio variant)
Count Capo d'Istria
Charles IX
Archduke Charles (Plate 88)
Princess Charlotte
Cardinal Consalvi (Plate 89)
Sir William Curtis (Plate 112)
Duke of Devonshire
Earl of Eldon
Francis, Emperor of Austria
Frederick William, King of Prussia
Baron von Gentz
George III (replica)
George IV (3 repetitions)
Princess Mary, Duchess of Gloucester
Prince von Hardenburg
Baron von Humboldt
Prince Leopold
Earl of Liverpool
Robert, Marquess of Londonderry (replica)
Donna Maria de Gloria, Queen of Portugal

Prince Metternich
Count Munster
Graf von Nesselrode
Gen. Ouvaroff
William Pitt (replica)
Pope Pius VII (Plate 90)
Count Platoff
Duc de Richelieu
Prince Schwarzenberg
Sir Walter Scott (Plate 109)
Princess Sophia (Plate 104)
Prince Tschernitsheff
Lord Thurlow (Plate 51)
Marquess Wellesley
Duke of Wellington
Sir Jeffrey Wyattville
Duke of York

BUCKINGHAM PALACE
George Canning (studio variant)
Caroline, Princess of Wales, and Princess Charlotte
Duke of Clarence
Prince George of Cumberland (Plate 117)
George IV

ST. JAMES'S PALACE
George IV

PUBLIC COLLECTIONS

BISHOPS AUCKLAND: THE PALACE
Hon. Shute Barrington, Bishop of Durham
William van Mildert, Bishop of Durham

BRISTOL: CITY MUSEUM AND ART GALLERY
Lady Caroline Lamb
A Lady

77

INDEX OF COLLECTIONS

INDEX OF COLLECTIONS

INDEX OF COLLECTIONS

BRITISH PRIVATE COLLECTIONS

INDEX OF COLLECTIONS

INDEX OF COLLECTIONS

INDEX OF COLLECTIONS

INDEX OF COLLECTIONS

INDEX OF COLLECTIONS

INDEX OF COLLECTIONS

EUROPE

PUBLIC COLLECTIONS

INDEX OF COLLECTIONS

INDEX OF COLLECTIONS

PRIVATE COLLECTIONS

INDEX OF COLLECTIONS

BIBLIOGRAPHY

A. BIOGRAPHICAL AND CRITICAL

D. E. WILLIAMS, *The Life and Correspondence of Sir Thomas Lawrence, Kt.*, 2 vols., London, 1831.

LORD RONALD SUTHERLAND GOWER, *Sir Thomas Lawrence*, London, 1900.

OSWALD G. KNAPP, *An Artist's Love Story*, London, 1904.

G. S. LAYARD, *Sir Thomas Lawrence's Letter Bag*, London, 1906.

SIR WALTER ARMSTRONG, *Lawrence*, London, 1913.

FRANZ BALKE, *Ein Kinderbildnis von Thomas Lawrence in der Österreichischen Galerie zu Wien* in *Formund Inhalt, Festschrift für Otto Schmidt*, Stuttgart, 1950.

DOUGLAS GOLDRING, *Regency Portrait Painter*, London, 1951.

CATALOGUES

ALGERNON GRAVES, Appendix to *Sir Thomas Lawrence* by Lord Ronald Sutherland Gower, London, 1900.

SIR WALTER ARMSTRONG, *Lawrence*, 1913.

REPRODUCTIONS

The Lawrence Gallery, Engravings from the Choicest Works of Sir Thomas Lawrence, P.R.A., London [Henry Graves & Co.], 1846.

Gowans Art Books, *The Masterpieces of Lawrence*, London and Glasgow, 1913: until now the only available collection of photographs of Lawrence portraits.

B. GENERAL

(1) GENERAL REFERENCE

F. O'DONAGHUE and H. M. HAKE, *Catalogue of Engraved British Portraits . . . in the British Museum*, 6 vols., London, 1908–25.

A. GRAVES, *A Century of Loan Exhibitions*, 1813–1912, 5 vols., London, 1913–15.

G. F. WAAGEN, *Treasures of Art in Great Britain*, 3 vols., London, 1854, *Supplement*, 1857.

W. T. WHITLEY, *Artists and their Friends in England*, 2 vols., London, 1928.

W. T. WHITLEY, *Art in England, 1800–1820*, London, 1928, and *Art in England, 1820–1837*, London, 1930.

(2) MEMOIRS, DIARIES AND HISTORIES

The number of books of this nature which contain interesting references to Lawrence is large, and I quote only some of those which relate anecdotes of importance, which quote letters, or which contain information relating to individual pictures which is not to be found elsewhere.

MADAME D'ARBLAY, *Diary and Letters* [Ed. C. Barrett], 8 vols., London, 1842–6.

A. ASPINALL (ed.), *The Letters of George IV*, 1812–1830, 3 vols., Cambridge, 1938.

C. F. BELL, *Annals of T. Banks*, Cambridge, 1938.

The Farington Diary (ed. J. Grieg), 8 vols. London, 1922–28.

LINDSAY FLEMING, *Memoir and Select Letters of Samuel Lysons*, Oxford (privately printed), 1934.

B. R. Haydon: Correspondence and Table-Talk [Ed. F. W. Haydon], 2 vols, London, 1876.

MRS. PAPENDIECK, *Court and Private Life in the time of Queen Charlotte* [Ed. Mrs. V. D. Broughton], London, 1887.

H. M. ROBINSON, *Coutts', The History of a Banking House*, London, 1929.

VITTORIA, DUCHESS OF SERMONETA, *The Locks of Norbury*, London, 1940.

REV. GORDON WOODGATE and G. M. G. WOODGATE, *A History of the Woodgates of Stonewall Park and Summerhill in Kent* (privately printed), 1910.

BIBLIOGRAPHY

BIBLIOGRAPHY

(3) CATALOGUES

ANON, *A Guide to Burghley House*, Stamford, 1815.

C. H. COLLINS BAKER, *Catalogue of Pictures in the Royal Collection at Windsor Castle*, London, 1937.

C. H. COLLINS BAKER, *Catalogue of British Paintings in the Henry E. Huntington Library and Art Gallery*, San Marino, California, 1936.

EARL BATHURST, *The Bathurst Collection of Pictures*, London (privately printed), 1908.

T. BORENIUS, *The Harewood Collection of Pictures*, Oxford (privately printed), 1936.

LIONEL CUST, *Eton College Portraits*, London, 1910.

MARTIN DAVIES, *National Gallery Catalogues, the British School*, London, 1946.

REV. EDMUND FARRER, *Portraits in Suffolk Houses (West)*, London, 1908.

R. W. GOULDING and C. K. ADAMS, *Catalogue of the Pictures belonging to the Duke of Portland*, Cambridge, 1936.

H. M. HYDE, *Londonderry House and its Pictures*, London, 1937.

MRS. R. L. POOLE, *Catalogue of Portraits in the University, etc., of Oxford*, Oxford, 3 vols, 1912–26.

G. SCHARF, *Catalogue of Pictures at Knowsley Hall*, London, 1875.

PRINCE DULEEP SINGH, *Portraits in Norfolk Houses*, 2 vols., Norwich, 1927.

LORD GERALD WELLESLEY and JOHN STEEGMAN, *The Iconography of the First Duke of Wellington*, London, 1935.

EVELYN, DUCHESS OF WELLINGTON, *Pictures and Sculpture at Apsley House*, 2 vols., London, 1901.

1. PHILADELPHIA HANNAH, LADY CREMORNE (c. 1740-1826)

249 × 145. R.A. 1789 (100)

Lt.-Cmdr. C. Windham, R.N. retd.

2. QUEEN CHARLOTTE (1744-1818)

239×147. R.A. 1790 (100)

By courtesy of the Trustees of the National Gallery, London

3. ELIZA FARREN, LATER COUNTESS OF DERBY (1759-1829)

238 × 147. R.A. 1790 (171)

Metropolitan Museum of Art, New York

4. SUSANNA COUNTESS OF OXFORD (1728-1804)

127 × 102. (*c.* 1790)

Sir Ian Forbes Leith, Bt.

5. LADY THEODOSIA VYNER (1765-1822)

127 × 102. R.A. 1791 (75)

Major E. R. F. Compton

6. THOMAS DAWSON, VISCOUNT CREMORNE (1725-1813)

249 × 145. (c. 1790)

Lt.-Cmdr. C. Windham, R.N. retd.

7. KING GEORGE III (1738-1820)

276×154. R.A. 1792 (65)

St. Mary's Guildhall, Coventry

9. MRS. CALVERLEY BEWICKE (*d.* 1859)

76×63. Before 1795

Frederick S. Ford

Reproduction—Courtesy Detroit Institute of Arts

8. LADY EMILY LENNOX, LATER LADY EMILY
BERKELEY (*d.* 1832)

76×63. R.A. 1791 (255)

Agatha, Lady Hindlip

10. LADY GEORGIANA APSLEY, LATER COUNTESS BATHURST
(*d.* 1841)

76 × 63. R.A. 1792 (150)

Earl Bathurst

12. JAMES, VISCOUNT HAMILTON (1786-1814)

76 × 63. R.A. 1790 (219)

Duke of Abercorn

11. HON. EMILY LAMB, LATER COUNTESS COWPER
(1787-1869) AND HON. HARRIET LAMB (died young)

76 × 63. R.A. 1792 (513)

Cowper Collection, Panshanger
By courtesy of Country Life

13. JOHN JULIUS ANGERSTEIN (1735-1823) AND HIS WIFE EMILY

256 × 159. R.A. 1792 (25)

Louvre, Paris
Courtesy Braun & Cie

14. LORD CHARLES TALBOT (1777-1849),
LATE SECOND EARL TALBOT, AND LORD JOHN TALBOT (1779-1825)

224 × 219

Earl of Shrewsbury

15. WILLIAM (1783-1812), ANNE (1787-1871), AND GEORGE HENRY (1784-1809)
CHILDREN OF LORD GEORGE CAVENDISH

245 × 210. R.A. 1790 (202)

Lord Chesham

17. SIR GILBERT HEATHCOTE (1773-1851)
76×63. R.A. 1791 (385)
Earl of Ancaster

16. HON. ARTHUR ANNESLEY (1785-1863) LATER
10TH VISCOUNT VALENTIA
76×63. (c. 1795)
Charles Finn Williams

18. ARTHUR ATHERLEY (*d*. 1844)

127 × 102. R.A. 1792 (209) *as Portrait of an Etonian*

Los Angeles County Museum

19. HOMER RECITING HIS POEMS

85 × 114. R.A. 1791 (180)

Major W. M. P. Kincaid-Lennox

20. WOODY LANDSCAPE

44 × 67. Before 1800

Col. H. M. Grant

21. LANDSCAPE: SOURCE OF THE MANIFOLD

44 × 67. Before 1800

Col. H. M. Grant

23. JOSEPH FARINGTON R.A. (1747-1821)

76 × 63. R.A. 1796 (164)

Formerly Miss Susan ffarington

22. WILLIAM LOCK OF NORBURY (1732-1810)

76 × 63. R.A. 1790 (19)

Museum of Fine Arts, Boston

25. WILLIAM, 2ND VISCOUNT BARRINGTON (1717-1793)

76 × 63. R.A. 1792 (109)

Viscount Barrington

24. REV. SAMUEL LYSONS (1730-1804)

76 × 63. 1796 -

Lindsay Fleming

26. CAPTAIN GRAHAM MOORE (1764-1843)

76 × 63. R.A. 1792 (366)

National Portrait Gallery

27. RABY WILLIAMS (1768-1808)

76 × 63. (c. 1793)

Mrs. J. Van Nostrand Dorr

28. GENERAL SIR CHARLES GREY (1729-1807), LATER FIRST EARL GREY

127 × 102. R.A. 1795 (131)

Earl Grey

29. RICHARD PAYNE KNIGHT (1750-1824)

127 × 102. R.A. 1794 (181)

Major W. M. P. Kincaid-Lennox

30. LADY CAROLINE HARBORD (*d.* 1850), LATER LADY SUFFIELD
127 × 102. R.A. 1793 (545)

Trustees of the XIth Marquess of Lothian

31. SARAH MOULTON BARRETT (1783-1795)

145 × 99. R.A. 1795 (75)

Huntington Gallery, San Marino (U.S.A.)

32. LADY LOUISA MANNERS (1745-1840), LATER COUNTESS OF
DYSART

248 × 155

J. D. Rockefeller Jr.

33. JOHN LORD MOUNTSTUART (1767-1794)

230 × 146. R.A. 1795 (86)

Marquess of Bute

34. FRANCIS HUMBERSTON MACKENZIE, 1st LORD SEAFORTH
(1754-1815)

236 × 145. R.A. 1798 (51)

Private Collection, France

35. SATAN SUMMONING HIS LEGIONS

432×271. R.A. 1797 (170)

Royal Academy of Arts

36. JOHN PHILIP KEMBLE (1757-1823), AS CORIOLANUS

287 × 178. R.A. 1798 (225)

Guildhall Art Gallery

38. SIR ANDREW SNAPE-HAMOND BT. (1738-1828)

76×63. Before 1806

Sir Egerton Hamond-Graeme, Bt.

37. GENERAL PASQUALE PAOLI (1725-1807)

76×63. R.A. 1799 (234)

W. H. Lee Ewart

39. MARGARET, LADY DUNDAS (1715-1802)

127 × 102. 1799

Marquess of Zetland

40. LORD GRANVILLE LEVESON-GOWER (1773-1846), LATER 1st EARL
GRANVILLE

239 × 145. (*c.* 1795-8)

Earl Granville

41. JOHN ALLNUTT (1773-1863)

240 × 142. R.A. 1799 (5)

Lt.-Cmdr. H. Sydney Egerton

43. MRS. SIDDONS (1755-1831)

76×63. Probably R.A. 1797 (166)

W. H. Lee-Ewart

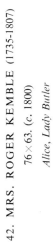

42. MRS. ROGER KEMBLE (1735-1807)

76×63. (c. 1800)

Alice, Lady Butler

45. *Possibly* SALLY SIDDONS (1775-1803)

76×63. (c. 1800)

By permission of the Trustees of the Wallace Collection

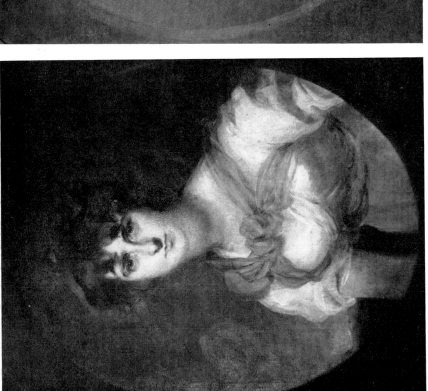
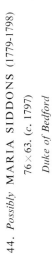

44. *Possibly* MARIA SIDDONS (1779-1798)

76×63. (c. 1797)

Duke of Bedford

47. HON. SOPHIA UPTON (*d.* 1853)

76×63. R.A. 1801 (173)

Formerly E. T. Stotesbury

46. HON. CAROLINE UPTON (*d.* 1862), LATER
MRS. JAMES SINGLETON

76×63. R.A. 1801 (190)

Formerly E. T. Stotesbury

48. MARY, LADY TEMPLETOWN (*d.* 1824) AND HER SON HENRY (1799-1863),
LATER 2ND VISCOUNT TEMPLETOWN

215 × 150. R.A. 1802 (5)

National Gallery of Art, Washington
By courtesy of the National Gallery of Art, Washington, D.C. Mellon Collection

49. JOHN PHILIP KEMBLE (1757-1823), AS HAMLET

305 × 198. R.A. 1801 (197)

Tate Gallery

By courtesy of the Trustees of the Tate Gallery, London

50. ELIZABETH, MARCHIONESS CONYNGHAM (1766/7-1861)

235 × 149. R.A. 1802 (176)

Trustees of the Londesborough Settled Estates

51. EDWARD, LORD THURLOW (1731-1806)

127×102. R.A. 1803 (21)

H.M. The Queen, Windsor Castle
By gracious permission of Her Majesty the Queen

52. CAROLINE, PRINCESS OF WALES (1768-1821)

127 × 102. 1804

National Portrait Gallery

54. HON. EMILY LAMB (1787-1869), LATER (I) COUNTESS
COWPER (2) LADY PALMERSTON

76 × 63. R.A. 1803 (127)

Cowper Collection, Panshanger

53. HON. WILLIAM LAMB (1779-1848), LATER 2ND
VISCOUNT MELBOURNE

76 × 63. (c. 1805)

Dowager Viscountess Hambleden

55. HON. THOMAS ERSKINE (1750-1823), LATER 1st LORD
ERSKINE

76×63. R.A. 1802 (184)

Lincoln's Inn

56. JOHN PHILPOT CURRAN (1750-1817)

76×63. 1800

Earl Grey

57. LADY ELIZABETH FOSTER (1759-1824), LATER DUCHESS OF
DEVONSHIRE

250 × 144. R.A. 1805 (195)

Courtesy of National Gallery of Ireland

58. FRANCES, MARCHIONESS OF BUTE (1773-1832)

236×145. 1806

Earl of Harrowby

59. MRS. MAGUIRE AND ARTHUR FITZ JAMES

165 × 165. R.A. 1806 (91) as *A Fancy Group*

Duke of Abercorn

60. SIR FRANCIS BARING, BT. (1740-1810), JOHN BARING (1730-1816), AND CHARLES WALL

156×210. R.A. 1807 (210)

Earl of Northbrook

62. HON. BERKELEY PAGET (1780-1842)

76×63. R.A. 1807 (17)

Lord Hylton

61. ROBERT, VISCOUNT CASTLEREAGH (1769-1822),
LATER MARQUESS OF LONDONDERRY

76×63. R.A. 1810 (61)

National Portrait Gallery

63. RT. HON. WILLIAM PITT (1759-1806)

127 × 102. R.A. 1808 (95)

Earl of Rosebery

64. WARREN HASTINGS (1732-1818)

91 × 71. R.A. 1811 (194)

National Portrait Gallery

65. MIRZA ABDUL HASSAN KHAN
91×71. 1810

William M. Chadbourne

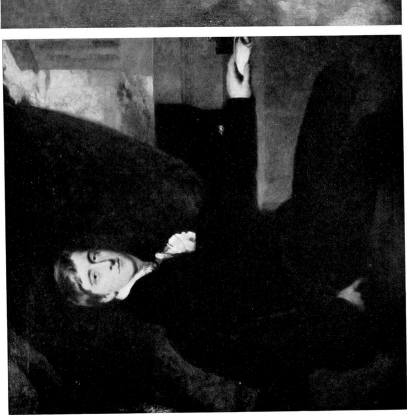

67. AYSCOGHE BOUCHERETTE, JR. (1792-1857)

76×63. (c. 1810)

Col. Michael Barne

66. WILLIAM, DUKE OF DEVONSHIRE (1790-1858)

145×119. 1812

Lord Dormer

68. SIR MARK MASTERMAN SYKES, BT. (1771-1823)
HENRIETTA, LADY SYKES (*d.* 1813) AND TATTON SYKES (1772-1863),
LATER 4TH BT.

236 × 181. Begun before 1806

Sir Richard Sykes, Bt.
By courtesy of Country Life

69. ANNE LUCY, LADY NUGENT (1790-1848)

238 × 148. Begun *c.* 1813

Major E. H. T. Boileau

70. MRS. GEORGE STRATTON

239 × 149. R.A. 1811 (69)

John and Mable Ringling Museum, Sarasota

71. ARTHUR, DUKE OF WELLINGTON (1769-1852)

91 × 71. *c.* 1814

Apsley House, London
Victoria and Albert Museum. Crown Copyright

72. LIEUT.-GEN. LORD CHARLES STEWART (1778-1854), LATER 3rd MARQUESS OF
LONDONDERRY

107 × 102. R.A. 1813 (159)

Marquess of Londonderry

74. ANTONIO CANOVA (1757-1821)

91×71. **R.A.** 1816 (184)

Gypsoteca Canoviana, Possagno

73. BENJAMIN WEST (1738-1820)

76×63. (c. 1811)

Amherst College, Mass.

75. JOHN JULIUS ANGERSTEIN (1735-1823)

92 × 71. R.A. 1816 (12)

Lloyd's

76. WILLIAM HENRY (1801-1832) AND JACOB PATTISON (1803-1874)
127 × 102. R.A. 1817 (44)

The National Trust, Polesden Lacy

77. MRS. JENS WOLFF (*d.* 1829)

127 × 101. R.A. 1815 (28)

Art Institute, Chicago

78. ROBERT GILMOR JR. (1774-1848)

76 × 63. 1818

Robert Gilmor Jr.
Courtesy Frick Art Reference Library, New York

79. MRS. ROBERT GILMOR, JR.

76 × 63. 1818

Mrs. Robert Gilmor, Sr.
Courtesy Frick Art Reference Library, New York

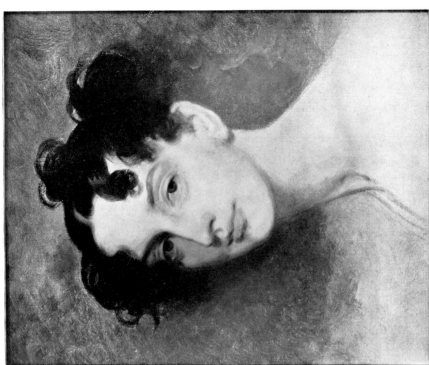

81. DOROTHEA, PRINCESS LIEVEN (1785-1857)

46×38. (c. 1815)

Tate Gallery

By courtesy of the Trustees of The Tate Gallery, London

80. MARIA, LADY CALLCOTT (1785-1842)

58×48. 1819

National Portrait Gallery

82. LYDIA ELIZABETH, LADY ACLAND (1786-1856) WITH HER SONS THOMAS
(1809-1898) AND ARTHUR (1811-1857)

154 × 118. R.A. 1818 (25)

Sir Richard Acland, Bt.

84. NAPOLEON, DUC DE REICHSTADT (1811-1832)

57×49. 1819

*Courtesy Fogg Art Museum, Harvard University,
Grenville Lindall Winthrop Collection*

83. PRINCESS MARIA THERESIA (1816-1867), LATER
QUEEN OF SICILY

79×63. R.A. 1820 (122)

Osterreichischen Galerie, Vienna

85. LADY SELINA MEADE (*d.* 1872), LATER COUNTESS 86. PRINCESS CLEMENTINE METTERNICH (1804-1820)
CLAM-MARTINICS AS *HEBE*
76×63. R.A. 1820 (140) 76×63. 1819

Earl of Clanwilliam *Formerly Prince Paul von Metternich-Winneburg*

87. H.R.H. THE PRINCE REGENT (1762-1830), LATER KING GEORGE IV

250 × 155. Replica of R.A. 1818 (61

Pinacoteca Vaticana

88. THE ARCHDUKE CHARLES (1771-1847)

270 × 176. 1818-19

H.M. The Queen, Windsor Castle
By gracious permission of Her Majesty The Queen

89. ERCOLE, CARDINAL CONSALVI (1757-1824)

269×178. 1819

H.M. The Queen, Windsor Castle
By gracious permission of Her Majesty The Queen

90. POPE PIUS VII (1742-1823)

264 × 146. 1819

H.M. The Queen, Windsor Castle
By gracious permission of Her Majesty The Queen

91. H.R.H. PRINCESS CHARLOTTE (1796-1817)

102 × 81. R.A. 1821 (70)

H.M. The King of the Belgians

92. MRS. HENRY BARING AND CHILDREN

198 × 198. R.A. 1821 (106)

Mrs. Ogden L. Mills

94. JOHN GEORGE LAMBTON (1792-1840), LATER 1st EARL
OF DURHAM

76×63. R.A. 1829 (135)

Earl of Durham

93. ARTHUR, DUKE OF WELLINGTON (1769-1852)

76×63. R.A. 1822 (134)

Private Collection

95. KING GEORGE IV (1762-1830)

265 × 175. 1822

By permission of the Trustees of the Wallace Collection

96. MARGUERITE, COUNTESS OF BLESSINGTON (1789-1849)

91 × 70. R.A. 1822 (80)

By permission of the Trustees of the Wallace Collection

97. ELIZABETH, LADY WALLSCOURT (1805-1877)

91 × 71. R.A. 1826 (65)

H. J. Joel

98. CHARLES WILLIAM LAMBTON (1818-1831)

141 × 110. R.A. 1825 (288)

Earl of Durham

99. EMILY (*d.* 1906) AND LAURA (*d.* 1894) CALMADY

77 × 71. R.A. 1824 (99)

Metropolitan Museum, New York

100. MARIE CAROLINE, DUCHESSE DE BERRI (1798-1870)

100 × 74. 1825

Mrs. John Wintersteen

101. JULIA, LADY PEEL (1795-1859)

91×71. R.A. 1827 (134)

Courtesy of the Frick Collection, New York

102. LADY GEORGIANA AGAR-ELLIS (1804-1860), LATER LADY DOVER, WITH
HER SON HENRY (1825-1866), LATER 3RD VISCOUNT CLIFDEN

127 × 102. R.A. 1828 (341)

Captain Charles Hepburn

103. JULIA PEEL (*c.* 1822-1893), LATER (1) COUNTESS OF JERSEY (2) MRS. CHARLES
BRANDLING

142×112. R.A. 1828 (77)

Sir George Cooper, Bt.

104. H.R.H. PRINCESS SOPHIA (1777-1848)

140×112. R.A. 1827 (57)

H.M. The Queen, Windsor Castle
By gracious permission of Her Majesty The Queen

105. MRS. BENJAMIN GOTT (*d.* 1857)

140 × 114. 1827

Mrs. P. M. Gott

107. FRANÇOIS, BARON GÉRARD (1770-1837)

76×63. 1825

Versailles
Courtesy Braun & Cie

106. SIR THOMAS LAWRENCE, P.R.A. (1769-1830)

91×69. (c. 1825)

Royal Academy of Arts

108. JOHN NASH (1752-1835)

138 × 110. R.A. 1827 (314)

Jesus College, Oxford

109. SIR WALTER SCOTT (1771-1832)

155 × 133. R.A. 1827 (146)

H.M. The Queen, Windsor Castle
By gracious permission of Her Majesty The Queen

110. ROBERT SOUTHEY (1774-1843)

142 × 112. R.A. 1829 (172)

National Gallery, Cape Town

112. SIR WILLIAM CURTIS (1752-1829)

90×70. R.A. 1824 (291)

H.M. The Queen, Windsor Castle
By gracious permission of Her Majesty The Queen

111. MRS. WILLIAM LOCK (1750-1832)

76×63. R.A. 1829 (455)

J. A. L. Smythies

113. LADY ROBERT MANNERS (1737-1829)

145 × 117. R.A. 1826 (75)

National Gallery of Scotland, Edinburgh

114. HENRY, 1st LORD BROUGHAN AND VAUX (1778-1868)

111 × 79. *c.* 1825

National Portrait Gallery

115. SIR ROBERT PEEL, BT. (1788-1850)

142×112. R.A. 1826 (101)

Earl Peel

116. DIANA, COUNTESS OF NORMANTON (*d.* 1841)

236 × 147. R.A. 1827 (75)

Earl of Normanton

117. PRINCE GEORGE OF CUMBERLAND (1819-1878)

254 × 140. 1828

H.M. The Queen, Buckingham Palace
By gracious permission of Her Majesty The Queen

119. WILLIAM WILBERFORCE (1759-1833)
96 × 109. Begun 1828
National Portrait Gallery

118. TOM MOORE (1779-1852)
76 × 63. R.A. 1830 (136)
Sir John Murray